Starmont Reader's Guide #58

WILLIAM GIBSON

Lance Olsen

Series Editor: Roger C. Schlobin

WILDSIDE PRESS

Biographical Note

Lance Olsen is author of two critical studies, *Ellipse of Uncertainty: An Introduction to Postmodern Fantasy* (1987) and *Circus of the Mind in Motion: Postmodernism and the Comic Vision* (1990); a novel, *Live from Earth* (1991); and numerous essays, short stories, and poems. He teaches at the University of Idaho.

This book, like all of them, is for Andrea

Published and copyright © 1992 by Starmont House, Inc., P.O. Box 851, Mercer Island, WA 98040. All rights reserved. International copyrights reserved in all countries. No part of this book may be reproduced in any form, except for brief passages quoted in reviews, without the expressed written permission of the publisher. Printed in U.S.A.

Contents

Acknowledgments/Abbreviations	v
Chronology and Canon	vii
1. Revolution, Revelation, and Rock'n'Roll	1
Who Was That Man?	1
Cyberpunk, Technosleaze, and the Apotheosis of Postmodernism	11
Twenty Minutes into the Future	20
Data Rustlers, Reptilian Brains, and Other Visionaries	28
Pyrotechnics and the Readerly Crisis	33
2. Burning Chrome	47
3. Neuromancer	63
4. Count Zero	85
5. Mona Lisa Overdrive	103
Primary Bibliography	115
Secondary Bibliography	117
Index	121

Acknowledgments

My warm thanks to Roger C. Schlobin and Ted Dikty for getting this ball rolling; the Fiction 2000 Conference at the University of Leeds (June-July 1989) for helping me to solidify and articulate my ideas at an important time in this book's development; William Gibson for reading and commenting upon this manuscript; and Andrea, my forever new romancer, for showing me that every day is fantastic.

Part of the argument in this book was developed in an essay that appeared in *Extrapolation* 32.3 (Fall 1991) under the title : "The Shadowed Spirit in William Gibson's Matrix Trilogy."

Cover Design Idea: by Andrea Olson

Abbreviations

BC	*Burning Chrome.* New York, 1986.
CZ	*Count Zero.* New York, 1986
MLO	*Mona Lisa Overdrive.* New York, 1988
N	*Neuromancer.* New York, 1984.
TDE	*The Difference Engine.* New York, 1991.

CHRONOLOGY AND CANON

1949: March 17, William Ford Gibson born in Conway, South Carolina.

1962-3: Attends boarding school in Tucson, Arizona, from which he is expelled.

1960's: Lives in Toronto, travels in Canada and Europe.

1972: Marries Deborah Jean Thompson and settles in Vancouver.

1976: Takes course on science fiction at University of British Columbia and writes his first story, "Fragments of a Hologram Rose."

1977: B.A. in English from University of British Columbia. "Fragments of a Hologram Rose" is published by a small Boston magazine, *Unearth*.

1981: "The Gernsback Continuum" appears in *Universe 11*, ed. by Terry Carr (New York: Doubleday); "The Belonging Kind" (with John Shirley) in *Shadows 4*, ed. Charles L. Grant (New York: Doubleday); "Johnny Mnemonic" in *Omni* (May); "Hinterlands" in *Omni* (October).

1982: "Burning Chrome" appears in *Omni* (July 1982).

1983: "Red Star, Winter Orbit" (with Bruce Sterling) published in *Omni* (July).

1984: *Neuromancer* published; "New Rose Hotel" appears in *Omni* (July).

1985: *Neuromancer* wins The Hugo, Nebula and Philip K. Dick awards; "Dogfight" (with Michael Swanwick) published in *Omni* (July).

1986: *Count Zero* appears; short stories collected in *Burning Chrome*; "The Winter Market" appears in the spring in *Vancouver Magazine, Interzone*, and *Stardate*.

1988: *Mona Lisa Overdrive* published.

1991: *The Difference Engine* (with Bruce Sterling) published.

Tomorrow is a lot weirder than we could ever imagine it to be.

—William Gibson

Revolution, Revelation, and Rock'n'Roll

This ain't rock'n'roll. This is GENOCIDE!
—David Bowie, "Diamond Dogs"

WHO WAS THAT MAN?

When *Neuromancer* appeared in July of the appropriately Orwellian year, 1984, William Gibson in many ways ceased being William Gibson. He became instead a shorthand for a way of thinking, feeling, and speaking. Academics viewed him, much to his chagrin, as the godfather of cyberpunk, an intriguing revolution in the arts directed against the lifeless neorealism and predictable science fiction of the late 1970's and early 1980's. They immediately set about creating a critical industry around him. Computer kids viewed him as a visionary and adopted his language, talked about his work, posted Gibsonesque messages on their computer bulletin boards, generated a real underground information network that Thomas Pynchon could only have dreamed about. A rock group, the Sonic Youth, dubbed themselves cyberpunks and featured a song called "The Sprawl" on its album, *Daydream Nation* (1988), while Kathy Acker, the postpunk godmother of the London fiction scene, wrote that parts of her novel, *Empire of the Senseless* (1988), are directly "ripped off" from *Neuromancer*.[1]

Not surprisingly, *Rolling Stone* and *The Village Voice* covered the phenomenon. But so did *The Wall Street Journal*, *People Weekly* and the *Times Literary Supplement*. In 1985, *Neuromancer* became the first novel to win science fiction's triple crown: the Hugo, Nebula, and Philip K. Dick awards. It also claimed the Ditmar, the top SF award given in Australia. Since then, it has been translated into a plethora of languages, including Catalan, Serbo-Croatian, and Japanese. Movie rights sold for $100,000, an impressive amount for a first novel. Epic Comics released volume one of *Neuromancer: The Graphic Novel* in 1989, with artwork by Bruce Jensen, script by Tom de Haven, and introduction by Gibson himself. By the end of the decade, Thomas Disch, writing in the *New York Times Book Review*, could take it for granted that Gibson is the "undisputed champion of cyberpunk."[2] Istvan Csicsery-Ronay, writing in the *American Book Review*, could claim that Gibson is "the most highly regarded young writer of U.S. SF."³ During the summer of 1989, about thirty scholars gathered for a conference at the University of Leeds; ostensibly they were to discuss trends in speculative fiction approaching the year 2000, but in fact their attention soon fixed on cyberpunk in general and William Gibson in particular.

One obviously can't help remembering Gibson's own observation tucked away like a prophecy near the opening of *Neuromancer*: "Fads swept the youth of the Sprawl at the speed of light; entire subcultures could rise overnight, thrive for a dozen weeks, and then vanish utterly" (chap. 4). Surely Gibson's work has produced its share of imitations at something approaching the speed of light, although this is greater testimony to his work's power and originality than to its trendiness. After all, in the last hundred years the same has been true of writers such as Hemingway, Joyce, Kafka, Barthelme, and Pynchon. Clearly, too, cyberpunk has turned out to be a vaguely defined and short-lived "movement" with few important figures in it, most of whom deny they are in fact cyberpunks. But, again, the same is true of such significant and influential twentieth-century "movements" as Imagism, Italian Futurism, and Minimalism.

The moment an artist comes under scholarly scrutiny, enters academic discourse, vitality begins to ebb. When critics begin quantifying and qualifying, something has run its course. Nonetheless, Gibson has transcended easy academic and generic boundaries. In a deeply felt way, he has reached many not usually interested in scholarly debates about the destiny of the planet or definitions of science fiction. Should he in fifty or a hundred years turn out to have fallen victim to his own prophecy, to have become no more than mere fad, it is scant comfort to contemporary readers poised uncertainly between two centuries. Currently there is no doubt that Gibson speaks powerfully to a large part of many people's desires, fears, and obsessions about such things as multinationals, global politics, computerized data, genetic engineering, cybernetics, techno-angst, and, ultimately, what it means to be human in an age that is infinitely complex, unnerving, and possibly posthuman.

Ironically, while profoundly interested in contemporary culture, the guru of cyberpunk is surprisingly uninformed and innocent about the nitty-gritty workings of contemporary technology. Famous for creating the cyberspace matrix in *Neuromancer* (1984), *Count Zero* (1986), and *Mona Lisa Overdrive* (1988), Gibson is the first to acknowledge "I have no grasp of how computers *really* work." He wrote his first novel on a manual typewriter with a broken key and tells the charming story of his first run-in with a computer. While writing *Count Zero*, he finally capitulated to contemporary culture, bought an Apple II, brought it home, and set it up. When he flipped it on, he thought it was malfunctioning because the external disk drive "started making this horrible sound like a farting toaster." He phoned the store, ready to complain, and was flabbergasted to learn that computers naturally made such noises. "Here I'd been expecting some exotic crystalline thing, a cyberspace deck or something," he says, and what I'd gotten was something with this tiny piece of a Victorian engine in it . . . . That noise took away some of the mystique for me, made it less *sexy* for me. My ignorance had allowed me to romanticize it."

Nor are computers the only technological devices Gibson finds a mystery. "Most of the time I don't know what I'm talking about when it comes to scientific or logical rationales that supposedly underpin my books," he confesses,[4] and Danny Rirdan has pointed out a number of Gibson's factual errors. In *Count Zero*, the walls of a space station are described as being stapled "with bulging loops of cable and fiber optic" (chap. 8), but fiber optic is the diameter of a strand of hair and a house would never be "bulging" with it.[5] Elsewhere, a company de-engineers computer chips to copy them, but the technology of engineering a chip is on a different scale from that of copying one; a company needn't do the former before doing the latter. Octagonal tablets appear often in Gibson's works, but an octagonal tablet, given its shape, would be particularly difficult to swallow, and hence a strange design.[6]

Such possible gaffes in no way devalue Gibson's work. Technological accuracy is not a litmus test for quality in imaginative writing. Simply because one cannot start a fire by channeling the sun's rays through eyeglasses prescribed for nearsighted people — a fact one of the characters in *Lord of the Flies* apparently forgets — in no way detracts from the emotional and philosophical power of Golding's immensely successful and important novel. Gibson's books are not about how microchips function (if they were, one might as well read a technical manual instead). They are about the implications of a data-obsessed, high-tech culture. As Gibson himself understands: "Part of my skill apparently lies in my ability to convince people I *do* know what I'm talking about. What I'm doing is just convincing lies — but lies that somehow manage to convey my own impressions of things, distorted for certain effects."[7] Gibson's art, as Picasso once said of his own, is a lie that tells the truth.

Gibson would prefer that readers concentrate on the art rather than the artist. He is reluctant to speak about his past, wary of discussing his own work, and would just as soon remain invisible as a person. This has partially been a consequence of the maddeningly high media profile he attained shortly after the publication of *Neuromancer*, partially a consequence of his naturally reticent personality. The result is that little biographical data about him is available. His friends don't like to talk about him. His interviews come to sound redundant, even slightly disingenuous. As Lewis Shiner notes: "He's made a lot of public statements in which he's simply said what he thought people wanted to hear . . . . So you want to take some of those interviews with lots of salt."[8]

Nonetheless, a number of facts are on the record about the writer his friends find genuinely thoughtful, sensitive, caring, and loyal. He was born in on March 17, 1948, and spent most of his childhood in the small town (so small, in fact, that it lacked a library) of Wytheville in southwestern Virginia. His family travelled frequently because his father, a contractor in the 1940's, moved from one construction job to another. According to Gibson, he found himself born into a science-fictional universe. His father's firm installed toilets for the Oak Ridge Project where the first atomic bombs were constructed. "Our family mythology was filled with wonderfully paranoid stories about how tight the security had been," he recalls. "I remember being told that each man on the project was required to observe and report on the actions of three other workers, and, of course, you knew that someone was watching you. That story was part of my world by the time I was, oh, five." Gibson also remembers the flood of media-SF during the early 1950s: cars trimmed like rockets, Captain Video on the television, "all kinds of wonderful toys I still recall with fondness — like Robby the Robot, who had a very small phonograph record in his chest and talked when you turned a crank. I remember that when Sputnik came along, it seemed to me to be somewhat after the fact."⁹

His father died when he was eight, his mother when he was a teenager at a boarding school in Tucson, Arizona. He returned to Virginia to discover his relatives didn't take kindly to his new, bohemian way of living. In 1968, vulnerable to the draft and using income from his parents' estate, he began travelling in Europe and Canada with Deborah, a Canadian who would become his wife, and who used to teach English as a second language in Vancouver. They settled in 1972. Gibson enrolled at the University of British Columbia as an English major after Deborah started working on her M.A. in linguistics. He became especially interested in studying critical methodologies. In 1977 he received his B.A.

Although he initially met science fiction when he was thirteen, reading such traditional SF writers as Robert Heinlein, Ray Bradbury and Theodore Sturgeon, it wasn't until his later teens that Gibson first encountered experimental SF in the form of William Burroughs, Thomas Pynchon, and J. G. Ballard. He took his first course on SF when he enrolled at UBC; he did so to pad his credits. The professor was Susan Wood, who had published essays on fantasy, SF, and Canadian literature, edited Ursula LeGuin's *The Language of Night* (1979), and put together the fantasy and SF issue of *Room of One's Own*, a feminist magazine published in Vancouver. She died in 1980. When Gibson informed her that he didn't have time to compose a term paper, she told him to write a short story instead. At first he thought he had discovered an easy out, but he worked on that piece of fiction for nearly three grueling months. In the end, he had thirteen pages to show: "Fragments of a Hologram Rose." He sent it to *Unearth*, a short-lived SF magazine that was first to publish Rudy Rucker and other cyberpunks, and *Unearth* accepted it. Upon the prompting of John Shirley, whom he had met at a science-fiction convention and with whom he had become friends, Gibson wrote his second story and sent it to *Omni*, which accepted it. Although for him writing is a "crazy, sloppy process with thousands of false starts and painful backtrackings," he claims he hasn't received a rejection slip since.¹⁰

Over the years, Gibson worked at various odd jobs. These include being a dishwasher at a French restaurant, a laborer at a fiberglass boat factory, and, significantly, a teaching assistant for a film history course at the University of British Columbia for three years. When Deborah and he had their children Graham and Claire, Gibson stayed at home to care for them. "I started writing while I was doing that," he says, "because it's one of the things you can do when you're home and the kids are asleep, and it doesn't cost anything."[11] But it was with reluctance that, now in his thirties, he returned to science fiction. He felt, he explains, he "was doing something regressive and pointless. I didn't expect to receive any recognition as an artist."[12] By his calculations, he had two counts against him: he was working in what many considered an insignificant genre, and, worse, he was trying to sabotage that genre by writing about the near future in a fairly experimental mode. So those outside the genre were sure to think him a hack, those inside a traitor. He was, of course, wrong. Recognition did come, and with a vengeance — not only in the form of the awards and film sale for *Neuromancer*, but also in the form of offers to do scripts for two of his early stories, "New Rose Hotel" and "Burning Chrome," as well as for *Alien III*. Gibson was baffled. "I thought I'd be addressing a very small audience," he says. "Writing science fiction seemed self-destructive, a willfully obscure thing to take up."[13]

More interesting than the biographical facts that accumulate around the writer, though, is the geography of his imagination. Partly because of his decision to become an expatriate by settling in Canada, Gibson's creative mind has become global rather than national. His fiction adopts an epic perspective. In the opening two pages of *Count Zero*, for instance, Turner visits no fewer than five countries. While Gibson's work regularly takes place in the Sprawl, Dog Solitude, Japan, or England, it also touches Greece, Turkey, India, Mexico, Singapore, Belgium, Spain, France, Canada, California, Arizona, Florida, and Virginia, not to mention high orbit. It conceives of the world, in other words, in postmodern terms. According to Gibson's geography, cultural identities have become neutralized. The international and intercultural have become the norm. He suggests it is thus grossly naive to think of oneself as an intellectual within any national restriction. This rhymes with Alvin Toffler's assertions in his futurist sociological study, *The Third Wave* (1980), which cyberpunk spokesperson Bruce Sterling calls "a bible to many cyberpunks."[14] Toffler argues that, as we approach a new millennium, globalism has become an "evolutionary necessity" for our planet and that it will be suicidal for us to pretend otherwise.[15]

If Gibson's imagination is deeply international, it is also deeply intertextual. Unlike many writers, he takes delight in naming works that echo through his own. He speaks with admiration of Ted Mooney's proto-cyberpunk novel, *Easy Travel to Other Planets* (1981), because it cites "all the sources [it has] plagiarized. He didn't say, copyright this, he said I stole this line."[16] For a writer like Gibson, the world is obviously less one of *plagiarism* than what Raymond Federman refers to as *pla(y)giarism*, a freeplay of suspension and acceptance, an acknowledgment that the universe is one of intertextuality where no one text has any more or less authority than any other. Writing becomes retro-writing. Language and ideas, like glass bottles and aluminum cans, become recyclable.

Literary intertextuality pervades his fiction. In interviews, he most often makes mention of Thomas Pynchon, whom he considers his "mythic hero." He sees Pynchon as "the start of a certain mutant breed of SF . . . that mixes surrealism and pop-cultural imagery with esoteric historical and scientific information . . . . If you talked with a lot of recent SF writers you'd find they've all read *Gravity's Rainbow* [1973] several times and have been very much influenced by it."[17] Next comes *William Burroughs' Naked Lunch* (1959), whose radical linguistic and formal experimentation Gibson embraces, though doesn't attempt to copy. Burroughs is liberating for Gibson for at least two reasons. First, he demonstrates that science fiction needn't be traditional in any sense of the word. Second, he shows that science fiction can explore the fringes of a culture, the criminal underground. From Alfred Bester — particularly *The Demolished Man* (1951) — Gibson inherits a tough energetic style, a techno-sleaze sensibility, and, in the figure of Gully Foyle, a decadent outlaw as protagonist. The hard-edged world of Samuel Delany (e.g., *Nova* [1968]), and the psychological explorations of J.G. Ballard (e.g., *The Atrocity Exhibition* [1969]) also surface in Gibson's fiction, and Carol McGuirk has convincingly shown that, in a more general way, Gibson borrows hard SF's interest in technology and soft SF's interest in selfhood.[18]

Gibson mentions two extra-SF literary influences as well: Dashiell Hammett (e.g., *The Thin Man* [1934]) and Robert Stone (e.g., *Dog Soldiers* [1973]). From both, he derives a hard prose and characters who maneuver at the edges of their cultures. From Hammett, he also borrows the detective figure whose primary form of power is information; this character becomes Gibson's computer hacker. From Stone, he adopts the vision of a morally bankrupt society filled with violence, drug addicts, and conspiracies.

Literary intertextuality is only part of the story. Equally important, if not more so, are influences from film, rock'n'roll, and other pop cultural centers. Steven Lisberger's *Tron* (1982), for example, prefigures the notion of cyberspace and is the first film to explore the computer hacker as techno-rebel, though the film clearly lacks the dirty feel of Gibson's worlds.[19] Many cyberpunks consider Ridley Scott's *Blade Runner* (1982) *the* cyberpunk film, filled as it is with hellish near-future landscapes and characters, but Gibson claims he went to see it about a third of the way through the first draft of *Neuromancer* and fled after thirty minutes because "it looked so much like the inside of my head."[20] He claims he never saw the rest of it. Both John Carpenter's *Escape from New York* (1981), set in 1997 when New York City has been converted into a maximum-security prison populated by the marginal, and David Cronenberg's *Videodrome* (1983), which explores the hallucinatory energy of mass media and corporate power, also clearly and directly feed Gibson's vision.

He considers the mood of his best fiction "the literary equivalent of the blues" but also acknowledges the strong presence of rock'n'roll's glitzy highspeed decadence in a story such as "The Winter Market."[21] He regularly mentions three sources in this context: Lou Reed (Gibson thought about using a line from the Velvet Underground's song, "Sunday Morning," as an epigraph for *Neuromancer*; Linda Lee is from the Velvet Underground's "Cool It Down"; a spaceship in *Count Zero* is named *Sweet Jane*); Steely Dan (Rikki Wildside in "Burning Chrome" was created with "Rikki Don't Lose that Number" in mind, as well as Reed's "Walk on the Wildside"; the bar is called the Gentleman Loser); and Bruce Springsteen (Gibson claims to have wanted to develop the same language of desire for computers that Springsteen has done for cars).

Gibson, then, is part of a generation raised on sensory overload. His imagination has been flooded by contemporary culture

— the Sex Pistols, terrorists, designer drugs, VCR's, CD's, MTV, AIDS, nuclear waste, oil spills — and has been intrigued by every moment of it. He is as comfortable with Mozart as with The Pretenders, Nabokov as *film noir*, Faulkner as fashion magazines, rock newspapers, the *New York Times*, *The Face*, *I-D*, clippings from *The New Scientist* that Bruce Sterling used to send him almost weekly, and comic books with their plot-led accent on a dark underworld peopled with easily identifiable types. Moreover, he has a strongly fashion-conscious eye. Shiner recounts how Gibson and he read *Thrasher*, a skateboard magazine, differently: "We talked on the phone about it, and I was raving about the attitude in the letter columns, and the way the cultural confrontation was set up between the skaters (running, essentially, on renewable energy sources) versus the rest of western civilization (i.e., cars), and how they were in competition for the one thing they both needed, which was concrete. Bill said, 'Yeah, but did you see those cool *shoes* on page 83?'"[22]

Most of his science fiction comes from simply paying attention to the world around him. As his friend and fellow SF writer Tom Maddox explains: "Gibson claims not to invent anything." This might at first seem a strange statement coming from a leading SF writer. But upon reflection it becomes less so. Gibson doesn't invent. He extrapolates. In our *fin-de-siècle* "reality" where Sperry Flight Systems in Arizona has already created a hypertrophic flight simulation system into which a pilot actually jacks, Nicholas Negroponte and Richard Bolt at MIT have generated a spacial data management system in which subjects maneuver among models of data, and Germany's Chaos Club has infiltrated NASA's mainframe while the Internet Worm has produced a virus in 6,000 computers from Berkeley to Massachusetts, Gibson needn't go far for his ideas. Maddox points out that "the concentrated tunnel vision of the videogames player mutates into *cyberspace*, the audio-visual intensity of color television and Walkman earphones into *simstim*, the password and data encryption programs of telecommunications into *ICE*, the Atlantic corridor into the *Sprawl*."[23]

Through this optic, Gibson is simply a realist in a culture where many people's preconceptions of what constitutes the impossible are assaulted every day. He is a postmodern writer who faces the problem of responding to a situation that is, literally, science fictional. Perhaps his use of the SF genre becomes clearer. "Science fiction can occasionally be looked at as a way of breaking through to history in a new way," Fredric Jameson has said. Science fiction achieves "a distinctive historical consciousness by way of the future rather than the past" and thus becomes "conscious of our present as the past of some unexpected future, rather than as the future of a heroic national past."[24] Science fiction teaches one to think about one's present situation by reframing it as the history of a future that hasn't yet occurred. Perhaps we may think of all science fiction (and certainly we may think of Gibson's) as a gloss upon the present, a mode of fiction that as a subset of the fantastic is designed to surprise, to question, and to put into doubt. "People have to live with things far grimmer and stranger than what's found in most science fiction. This," Gibson says, "*is* the future."[25]

CYBERPUNK, TECHNOSLEAZE, AND THE APOTHEOSIS OF POSTMODERNISM

Jameson's comment accords well with that of Darko Suvin who, in his by-now famous phrase, defines science fiction as the "literature of cognitive estrangement."[26] Through its various techniques, science fiction makes the world *strange*, distorts it, and, by doing so, allows the reader to see the universe anew. Science fiction confronts the reader with otherness, with alien characters and landscapes, which readers recognize as extensions of themselves and their contemporary cosmos. Consequently, it enacts the process Russian Formalists, such as Victor Shklovsky, call *defamiliarization*. It disrupts conventional perception, sometimes to a lesser extent, sometimes to a greater, thereby forcing us to perceive our situation in a fresh way. It interrogates traditional notions of reality, selfhood, and language, challenging conventional ideas of ontology and epistemology. Very little, if any, science fiction actually tells about the future, however. Most tells about the present — about contemporary culture's anxieties, wishes, fixations. "Readers who think that sf is 'about' the future are naive," Gibson reminds us.[27] "I don't think science fiction has a lot of predictive capacity, but it's an interesting tool for looking at the world you live in."[28]

Obviously science fiction has *some* predictive capacity, though, in the sense that it is a narrative mode that focuses our attention on things (possibly) to come. It debates what is important to contemplate, thereby orienting readers with respect to the future. It asks the reader to be forward thinking, to ponder the relationship between what is and what might be, and it thereby invites consideration of tomorrow. Its extrapolations from the present about such concerns as artificial intelligence, nuclear power, and postindustrial politics become, not literal predictions, but figurative warnings. *This is what might happen*, it often asserts, *if we do not think harder.*

Gibson is less interested in exactly what will happen in the year 2050 than he is with what is happening today. Or, more precisely, he is interested in how today is already tomorrow in a world undergoing future shock. "I'll be sitting in the Dallas/Ft. Worth Airport looking out my window and thinking, 'What *is* this landscape?'" he explains. "You know you're in a very strange place, but you're also aware this weirdness is just your world. One of the liberating effects that SF had on me when I was a teenager was precisely its ability to tune me in to all this strange data and make me realize that I wasn't as totally isolated in my perception of the world as monstrous and crazy."[29]

Because of this stress on a future-present, Gibson does not think of himself primarily as a science-fiction writer. He feels the label "science fiction," often applied to his work, is simply a helpful marketing strategy that has allowed his fiction to reach a wider audience than it might have done otherwise. "As far as I know, I've reached exactly the audience that I would have wanted to reach, plus the science fiction audience as well," he says. "If you're selling reasonably well as a science fiction writer in the States these days, you're getting quite a lot of exposure . . . . And I think if I'd been writing these books and publishing them as sort of *avant-garde* mainstream literature, relatively few people would have heard of them."[30]

His association with cyberpunk, a term which spawned much heated debate in the SF community in the late 1980s, certainly hasn't hurt his popularity any. It has been, as he is quick to acknowledge, "good for business." Despite his assertations that, "historically speaking, I'm not sure there is, or even was, a movement in . . . the capital 'M' sense of the word," and that "I've sort of gotten tired of [talking about] it," Gibson's name has become inextricably linked with cyberpunk.[31] Csicsery-Ronay has gone so far as to write that "my suspicion is that most of the literary cyberpunks bask in the light of one major writer who is original and gifted enough to make the whole movement seem original and gifted. That figure is William Gibson, whose first novel, *Neuromancer*, is to my mind one of the most interesting books of the postmodern age."[32]

To gain a fuller contextual understanding of Gibson's work, it is necesary to spend some time discussing the history and major tenets of cyberpunk. Although what may finally matter most are the differences and not the similarities among the loose group of writers whose names are connected with cyberpunk, it is nonetheless significant that, during the mid-1980's they viewed themselves as belonging to a movement that shared a vaguely defined if deeply felt sensibility. As late as 1986, many of the key figures were quite happy to contribute to Sterling's *Mirrorshades: The Cyberpunk thology*, which Sterling prefaces with what amounts to a cyberpunk manifesto. On the one hand, the cyberpunks are wary of "label mongering" because of the pigeonholing effect labels tend to have on creator.[33] On the other, they are mesmerized by labels because of the powerful space labels open in literary discourse. Thus these writers have tried on, or have had applied to them against their wishes, a number of labels including The Outlaw Technologists, The Neuromantics, and The Mirrorshades Group — these in addition to "The Cyberpunks" which, according to a *Science Fiction Eye* editorial, was originally coined by Gardner Dozois in an article in the *Washington Post*.[34] Even after "cyberpunk," whose usefulness as a term might have run its course by 1988 or 1989, many still think of themselves as part of something simply referred to as The Movement.

At the core of the literary cyberpunks stand Rudy Rucker (*Software*, 1982), Lewis Shiner (*Frontera*,1984), John Shirley (*Eclipse*, 1985), Greg Bear (*Blood Music*, 1985), and Pat Cadigan (*Mindplayers*, 1987) — as well, of course, as Sterling (*The Artificial Kid*, 1980) and Gibson. Work by Tom Maddox, Marc Laidlaw, James Patrick Kelly, and Paul di Filippo also appears in Mirrorshades, while such seemingly dissimilar writers as John Brunner, George Alec Effinger, Richard Kadrey, and even Kathy Acker have at one time or another been associated with the cyberpunks, at least in the minds of literary critics. In retrospect, *Blade Runner* (1982) and *Videodrome* (1983) stand as cinematic cyberpunk classics. So do such pop cultural projects as the *Max Headroom* televison show, MTV videos and station ID's at their most innovative, and the self-destructive robotic sculptures of Mark Pauline and the Survival Research Laboratories.

Common to manifesto pronouncements, Sterling asserts something new and fresh (cyberpunk) has just begun to revolt against something old and stale (conventional jaded 1970s science fiction). On closer inspection, it becomes apparent that cyberpunk has done no more than develop trends already present in a number of previous texts, such as those by New Wave writers like Harlan Ellison, Samuel Delany, Philip K. Dick, Brian Aldiss, and J. G. Ballard. David Bowie in his Ziggy Stardust pose, Laurie Anderson, and Devo also figure into the cyberpunk equation. One of the most influential earlier sources has, of course, been the work of Thomas

Pynchon, for whom the cyberpunks hold "special admiration." Pynchon's "integration of technology and literature stands unsurpassed."[35]

Integration is a key concept in cyberpunk. "Suddenly a new alliance is becoming evident: an integration of technology and Eighties counterculture," Sterling remarks. "An unholy alliance of the technical world and the world of organized dissent — the underground world of pop culture, visionary fluidity, and street-level anarchy."[36] And again: "cyberpunk comes from the realm where the computer hacker and the rocker overlap, a cultural Petri dish where writhing gene lines splice."[37] Integration is even enacted in the neologism *cyberpunk*. *Cyber* connotes the techno-sphere of *cyber*netics, *cyber*nauts, electronics, and computers. This is coupled with *punk* connotations of the countercultural socio-sphere, especially late 1970's punk rock, itself an embodiment of both anarchic violence and an attempt to return to the roots of pure rock'n'roll. At the heart of cyberpunk is the conviction that, like rock'n'roll, science fiction had become too safe during the mid-1970s, that drastic measures were required to reenergize it. This project shares much with that of the New Wave that appeared a generation before and attempted to add literary craftsmanship, power, and innovation to what it perceived as the lifeless and predictable pulp science fiction preceding it.

While the romantic counterculture of the late 1960's was in large part anti-tech, postmodern cyberpunk is high-tech. "Technology is visceral," Sterling states, and Timothy Leary adds that personal computers are the "LSD of the 1980s." Cyberpunks feel, not that they are just working in a literary tradition of science fiction, but that they have been born into a world where technology is "pervasive, utterly intimate. Not outside us, but next to us. Under our skin; often, inside our minds."[38]

The most striking emblem of cyberpunk integration are the mirrorshades, mirrored sunglasses, which became the movement's totem in 1982. "The reasons for this are not hard to grasp," Sterling explains. "By hiding the eyes, mirrorshades prevent the forces of normalcy from realizing that one is crazed and possibly dangerous. They are the symbol of the sun-staring visionary, the biker, the rocker, the policeman, and similar outlaws."[39] Mirrorshades depersonalize and dehumanize, giving world rather than self back to the viewer; this reflects cyberpunk's emphasis on moral neutrality and emotionless surface. Mirrorshades suggest that the future is opaque to us all, that at best in cyberpunk fiction is a reflection of the present. Traditionally in Western art, eyes have been windows to the soul, insight, and love; in cyberpunk, however, eyes are covered with reflective surfaces (Bobby Newmark in *Count Zero* wears mirrorshades; Molly has had them surgically implanted into her face), or are often plainly artificial (Rikki in *"Burning Chrome"* buys Zeiss Ikon eyes modelled on those of her favorite simstim star). Western tradition is thereby turned on its head. Human and inhuman merge. Humanism gives way to posthumanism. Man becomes — to use the title from Anthony Burgess's proto-cyberpunk novel (1963) — a clockwork orange.

Cyberpunk, forced as it is by the press of fashion to present itself as radically new, seems unaware that it shares much with an earlier multimedia movement in the twentieth century: Italian Futurism. Initially a literary concept born in the mind of the poet Filippo Tommaso Marinetti and best expressed in the works of Umberto Boccioni, Futurism was propagated in manifestos in 1909 and 1910. Its proponents attacked ideas of imitation, harmony, good taste, and traditional subject matter embodied in libraries, museums, academies, and cities of the past, while extolling the beauties of revolution, war, metamorphosis, motion, and, most important, the speed and dynamism of modern metropolitan life, industry, and technology. From the German Expressionists, it also inherited a passion for developing an empathetic identity between the viewer/reader and the artwork, a direct appeal to emotions. In his manifesto of "tumbling and incendiary violence," Marinetti "sing[s] the love of danger," "the beauty of speed, ... the great crowds tossed about by work, by pleasure, or revolt,... the gluttonous railway stations..., the factories hung from the clouds ..., and the gliding flight of airplanes."[40] Italian Futurists display the same adoration of the contemporary, of speed and motion and technology tinged with danger, as do the cyberpunks. One cannot help thinking of Marinetti, for example, when reading about Turner closing his eyes and jacking into the microsoft carrying Mitchell's dossier in *Count Zero:* "It came on . . . , a flickering, nonlinear flood of fact and sensory data, a kind of narrative conveyed in surreal jump cuts and juxtaposition. It was vaguely like riding a roller coaster that phased in and out of existence at random, impossibly rapid intervals, changing altitude, attack and direction with each pulse of nothingness" (chap. 3).[41]

It is easy enough to attack cyberpunk, or what some less charitable critics have dubbed *cyberbunk* or *cyberjunk*, on a number of predictable fronts. Interestingly enough, few choose to take on the truth-value of its vision. Most, such as Gregory Benford and David Brin, primarily launch assaults along media hype lines. "What we have here, folks," Benford declares, "is a marketing strategy masquerading as a literary movement."[42] Brin chimes in: "'cyberpunk' is nothing more or less than the best publicity gimmick to come to Speculative/Fiction in years. Adherents make their grand pronouncements and thereby attract the roving press flocks, always eager to do a piece on the latest rebel."[43] Others, such as John Kessel and Csicsery-Ronay, primarily launch assaults along narrative lines: "How many formulaic tales can one wade through," the latter asks, "in which a self-destructive but sensitive young protagonist with an (implant/prosthesis/telechtronic talent) that makes the evil (megacorporations/police states/criminal underworlds) pursue him through (wasted urban landscapes/elite luxury enclaves/eccentric space stations) full of grotesque (haircuts... /rock music/sexual hobbies/designer drugs ...) representing the ... mores ... of modern civilization in terminal decline?"[44] Cyberpunk falls into the trap of virtually all movements: it is by nature trendy, its spokesperson shrill. It opposes itself to a tradition out of which it in fact grew. It is short-lived. Its few powerful key works are relatively easy to imitate, if not equal.

None of this negates the fact that cyberpunks (self-proclaimed and otherwise such as Gibson, David Bowie, Ridley Scott, Laurie Anderson, and Kathy Acker, continue to address immensely important contemporary matters in an intensely forceful and innovative way. "Cyberpunk," Larry McCaffery observes, "seems to be the only art systematically dealing with the most crucial political, philosophical, moral, and cultural issues of our day."[45] Among those issues that go virtually unnoticed by other contemporary creators are genetic engineering, organ transplantation, multinational control of computer networks (and thus information access), commoditization of culture, future shock, artificial intelligence, cybernetics, chemical weapons, terrorism, techno-angst, the devaluation of cash currency, conurbanization, the advent of postindustrialism, denationalization, hacker outlaws, religious cults, the reemergence of fundamentalism around the world, toxic waste, famine, and American culture's romanticization of insanity. Such concerns seem simple "publicity gimmicks" or mere "trendiness" only to the wildly naive or amazingly uninformed.

Many cyberpunk ideas about these issues were influenced by Toffler's *The Third Wave* (1980), a generally optimistic futurist sociological study that in tone and vision is a far cry from Gibson's fiction.[46] Toffler argues that civilization has evolved through three stages or "waves." The First Wave, reaching back at least ten-thousand years, was agricultural. The Second Wave, initially surfacing in the seventeenth century, was industrial. This "indust-reality" advocated standardization, specialization, massification, centralization, concentration, nationalization, and synchronization. Since the 1950s, a Third Wave has appeared and begun to clash violently with the Second. Presently "colliding visions rock our mental universe" as the world teeters between opposing perceptions of reality.[47] The Third Wave has begun to revolutionize the deep structure of society, entering the techno-, info-, socio-, bio-, power- and psycho-spheres, and advocating the antithesis of "indust-reality": customization, decentralization, demassification, diversification, and globalization. Rather than thinking in terms of hierarchy, it thinks in terms of network. Rather than thinking in terms of Cartesian parts, it thinks in terms of post-Cartesian wholes. Politically, it moves away from the authoritarianism of capitalism or socialism toward a complex democracy advocating minority power and denationalization. Third-Wave civilization will be neither utopia nor dystopia. It will be *practopia* instead — "neither the best nor the worst of all possible worlds, but one that is both practical and preferable to the one we had."[48]

Informed by Toffler's ideas, cyberpunk harmonizes well with the basic orientation of postmodernism. Csicsery-Ronay has in fact called cyberpunk "the apotheosis of postmodernism."[49] While power struggles continue to rage around the definition of this term and its parameters continue to shift almost weekly, some agreement has nonetheless been reached about the mode of consciousness many seem intent on naming *postmodernism*. Like Toffler's Third Wave, it embraces notions of decentralization, diversification, and demassification. Like cyberpunk, it has little patience with borders — between human and machine, country and country, writer and writer. As I have discussed at length in *Ellipse of Uncertainty* and *Circus of the Mind in Motion*, postmodernism may be thought of as a radical form of skepticism that challenges all we once took for granted about language and experience. This definition subsumes a number of seminal ones: incredulity toward overarching belief systems (Lyotard); an inability to reflect and shape the world (Thiher) or self (Caramello); ontological instability (McHale); cultural schizophrenia (Baudrillard); the fusion and confusion of "high" and "low" culture (Huyssen).[50]

Implicit in modern thought, as Gianni Vattimo writes, is the belief that history is progressive. The world, according to such modern thinkers as Hegel and Marx, undergoes a series of relatively gradual revolutions (political, aesthetic, intellectual, etc.) *towards* something. In consumerized postmodern thought, however, the new is taken for granted. We no longer generate the new in order to "progress." Rather, we are addicted to producing it for its own sake. Revolution follows on the heels of revolution, but leads nowhere.[51] "Accustomed to coping with low diversity and slow change, individuals and institutions suddenly find themselves trying to cope with high diversity and high-speed change," Toffler affirms. "The cross-pressures threaten to overload their decisional competence. The result is future shock."[52]

Postmodern humanity must learn to deal with a situation that goes nowhere, but travels at an astonishing velocity. Alan Wilde claims the truly postmodern human will come to accept extreme indeterminacy as a way of life, John Brunner (deeply influenced by Toffler) that one must "adjust to shifts of fashion, the coming-and-going of fad-type phrases, the ultrasonic-blender confusion of twenty-first-century society, as a dolphin rides the bow wave of a ship . . . . and have a hell of a good time with it."[53] Often, of course, this joy in the face of unlimited possibility seems forced, paired as it is with the feeling that something important has been irrevocably lost. Such paradoxes, or contradictions, lie at the heart of the postmodern enterprise and remain, as Linda Hutcheon points out, forever unresolved.

Cyberpunk, then, is a cultural manifestation of postmodernism. With this in mind, Brian McHale's observation comes as no surprise:

over the past few decades postmodernism has begun borrowing motifs and *topoi* from science fiction in works such as Alasdair Gray's *Lanark* (1981) and Raymond Federman's *The Twofold Vibration* (1982), while science fiction has begun doing the same with postmodernism in works such as J. G. Ballard's *The Atrocity Exhibition* (1969) and Samuel Delany's *Dhalgren* (1974).[34] It depends on the vantage point as to how Gibson fits into this paradigm. From many readers' perspective, he is a science-fiction writer who has adapted several postmodern motifs and *topoi* to his purposes. From Gibson's own perspective, he is a postmodern writer who has adapted several science-fiction motifs and *topoi* to his purposes. In either case, the result is the creation of a fictional universe and core of central themes that are both alarming and intriguing.

TWENTY MINUTES INTO THE FUTURE

Much conventional science fiction, such as Isaac Asimov's *Foundation* trilogy (1951-1953), is typically set in the distant future, peopled with aliens, and enacted on a galactic and heroic scale. Gibson's science fiction, on the other hand, extrapolates an all-too-real near-future world that is set as little as twenty or thirty years from now, peopled with those at the margins of society, and enacted on a global and antiheroic scale. Uncomfortable with the safety that traditional science-fiction's distance in time, strange creatures, and cosmic scope creates, Gibson limns the decadent and dystopic universe of late capitalism filled with powerful amoral multinational corporations, pollution, urban sprawl and designer drugs. He sees no reason to predict the unknowable far future which, as in a film such as *Star Wars* (1977), often comes to resemble the chivalric past of romance where goodness, stability, and order prevail in a better-than-life universe dominated by ideals of courage and honor. Gibson bases his world on contemporary reality that for him is "more accurate in an iconic sense than as a map of where we're going."[55]

Like Faulkner and his Yoknapatawpha County, Gibson creates a single fictional universe for many works. Its geography and time frame are often deliberately vague. The reader often has the impression that civilization has already peaked, that there's nowhere to go but down. World War III has occurred, apparently lasting only three weeks and centered in Bonn and Beograd. Because of a pandemic, horses are extinct. Printed books have become fashionably archaic, and the most popular entertainment now takes the form of simstims or Simulated Stimuli, whereby jacking into a machine one can experience the sensations and perceptions of another person. Paper money, now quasi-illegal, has been replaced for the most part by credit chips. Children, suggestive of innocence, are virtually absent, while claustrophobia, produced by rampant overpopulation, abounds; Kumiko in *Mona Lisa Overdrive* moves through "crowd-river[s]" (chap. 11) and is startled when, almost thirteen years old, she sees her first empty street.

Having entered Bobby's cyberspace unit in *Mona Lisa Overdrive*, Slick Henry and Thomas Trail Gentry discover themselves walking through Straylight with a floor, reminiscent of one of Julian

Schnabel's neoexpressionist works or Antoni Gaudí's neo-Gothic Guell Park, fashioned from shattered china and epoxy. "Thousands of different patterns and colors in broken bits," Slick thinks, "but no overall design in how it had been put down, just random" (chap. 31). This serves as well as a description of Gibson's universe: fractured, confused, contingent, constructed of *gomi* (Japanese for *garbage*). A larger version of this is found in The Sprawl, the conurbation officially known as BAMA, the Boston-Atlanta Metropolitan Axis. In this "vast generic tumble that was [the twenty-first] century's paradigm of urban reality," trash overflows in the sidewalks, ruined buildings line the streets, and damaged geodesic domes inadvertently producing microclimates of drizzle and lightning look like Giovanni Piranesi's prison sketches (*MLO* chap. 22).

Pollution pervades the scene. The Sprawl has a "signature smell, a rich amalgam of stale subway exhalations, ancient soot, and the carcinogenic tang of fresh plastics, all of it shot through with the carbon edge of illicit fossil fuels" (*CZ* chap. 16). As early as Gibson's first story, "Fragments of a Hologram Rose," acid rain — "sour," "the color of piss" — forces the protagonist to don respirator and goggles to go outside. A poison administered to roaches to exterminate them has instead transformed them into mutants. Dead fish wash up on filthy Floridian shores. Dog Solitude stands as an emblem of it all: once a toxic landfill operation, it is now a vast rusty red wasteland where nothing grows, the water packed with PCB's is undrinkable, and no animals can live except birds who must go elsewhere to feed.

Japan, which Gibson initially visited only when delivering the manuscript of *Mona Lisa Overdrive* to his publishers there in 1988, dominates this fictional universe. Initially appearing in "Fragments of a Hologram Rose," where the protagonist, Parker, is indentured to the American subsidiary of a Japanese plastics combine when fifteen years old, Japan appears at every level from major settings to various seemingly insignificant background noise: stim-star magazines in Baltimore are written in Japanese, spacesuits and bathtub filtration devices are made by Japanese companies, and space shuttles play Japanese music. The prevalence of such Orientalia is partially the result of Gibson playing on a deep-seated American fear — that future global power probably won't be centered in America. But it also marks the gradual realization on the part of

Americans that, as Grania Davis has pointed out in her foreword to a collection of Japanese science-fiction stories, "the Japanese are already living in a version of the future — with its overcrowding, micro-electronic gadgets, polluted environment, and efficient group-minds. The problems — and solutions — of the future are happening in Japan right *now*."[56] For Gibson, Japan is tomorrow happening today.

If Gibson imagines a frightening external universe in the Sprawl, Dog Solitude, and Japan, he imagines a mesmerizing internal one in the cyberspace matrix. Essentially "an abstract representation of the relationships between data systems," as the narrator of "Burning Chrome" explains, the cyberspace matrix surrounds the jacked-in computer programmer with "bright geometries representing ... corporate data ... [The cyberspace matrix is] the electronic consensus-hallucination that facilitates the handling and exchange of massive quantities of data." Although Porush and others maintain Gibson's matrix is an extrapolation of spacial data management systems now being studied at MIT, NASA, and elsewhere, Gibson says the idea actually came to him while walking down Granville Street in Vancouver. He saw kids playing in video arcades and noticed "in the physical intensity of their postures how *rapt* these kids were ... And these kids clearly *believed* in the space these games projected."[57]

Originally no more than an abstract representation of data in his early stories and first novel, cyberspace metamorphoses over the course of Gibson's matrix trilogy. At the moment the two artificial intelligences, Neuromancer and Wintermute, merge at the end of Gibson's first novel, becoming a god-like unity of opposites, the newly generated entity fragments because it is lonely and wants to have some fun with itself. The result is the birth of a host of smaller gods or subprograms in the matrix that take on the names of voodoo deities. The idea for these came from an article on Haitian voodoo Gibson read in *National Geographic*. "It seemed to me that the underlying beliefs [of voodoo] were very appropriate to a computer society," he says. "With voodoo, the big God is very far away and totally unconcerned with mere human beings. Between you and the big God is a pantheon of greedy, lustful, sharp-operator gods, who are all part of a big, incestuous family."[58]

Gibson thus blends notions of religion and technology in cyberspace. But, just like the video arcades which initially spawned the matrix, both religion and technology are shown to be no more than games, abstract organizations of data that at best bear a distant relationship with reality. Perhaps the gods in the matrix are real. Perhaps they are no more than virus programs that have gotten loose in the matrix and replicated. Either they exist, or they don't. Or, from a different perspective, perhaps they both exist and do not exist simultaneously. That is to say, as Lucas observes in *Count Zero*, perhaps they have taken on the function of metaphor. "When Beauvoir or I talk to you about the loa and their horses . . . you should pretend that we are talking two languages at once," Lucas tells Bobby. "One of them, you already understand. That's the language of street tech . . . . But at the same time, with the same words, we are talking about other things, and *that* you don't understand" (chap. 16). Some need to organize their world using the language of religion, others the language of technology. Technology becomes a religion, religion a technology.

Although the existence of the alternate universe of cyberspace raises questions about the relationship between religion and technology, Gibson had other intentions in mind when creating it. For him, cyberspace is a metaphor for memory. Computer memory suggests both individual and cultural memory — and the fragility of both. At the same time, the matrix functions as a metaphor for the enormously complex linkages of the global information system, and for the mass media itself that acts as a drug on our culture's consciousness. According to Gibson, all one needs to do to arrive at such a reading is "think about someone completely immersed in television, watching a giant high-resolution screen, wearing Walkman earphones with the sound cranked up really loud, sitting close enough to the TV to have a total experience . . . On one level, cyberspace is a metaphor for the media world that forms a dangerously large part of some people's reality."[59]

The gothic quality of the cyberspace matrix, haunted by voodoo gods and spirits of the dead, implies as well the surreal landscape of the irrational psyche, which itself implies a metaphor for mind/body dualism. Characters who enter cyberspace leave their bodies behind, lose themselves in the mental landscape of the matrix. Case, for instance, lives for the "bodiless exultation of cyberspace" while exhibiting "a certain relaxed contempt for the flesh." For him "the body was meat." When he steals from his employers, they retaliate by damaging his nervous system with mycotoxin which dulls his edge at the computer console. Case perceives this as a "Fall" from grace that forces him to remain locked in "the prison of his own flesh" (*N* chap. 1).

Discussing the makeup of Gibson's external and internal universes soon evolves into a consideration of his central themes. If cyberspace is a metaphor for individual and cultural memory, then, clearly Gibson intimates that we continually reprogram or rewrite our memories. In the world according to Gibson, history becomes fiction. Many of his characters, such as Kumiko and Molly, exhibit a certain nostalgia for a past they have rewritten almost beyond recognition. In "Red Star, Winter Orbit," Colonel Korolev, the first man on Mars, can't recall what actually happened during his historic voyage; all he can recollect are the videotapes of the experience. Sandii in "New Rose Hotel" tells her past differently to the narrator each time it comes up.

Memory, no matter how faulty, is information. Information is power. The person who controls the data flow controls the game. Consequently, Swain in *Mona Lisa Overdrive* redistributes intelligence he acquires from 3Jane, thus converting it into control, and Johnny Mnemonic in Gibson's early story knows that "we're an information economy. They teach you that in school. What they don't tell you is that it's impossible to move, to live, to operate at any level without leaving traces, bits, seemingly meaningless fragments of personal information. Fragments that can be retrieved." To let others know about you is to let others control you. Information wields power greater than monetary or military force.

Multinational corporations control most information and hence dominate the landscape of Gibson's fiction. The production of original information is no longer the province of one mind, as it was in the nineteenth and early twentieth centuries (Frankenstein, Bell, Einstein). Now it is the province of a collective. Reminiscent of megacompanies like IG Farben and Yoyodyne that make up Them in Pynchon's universe, entities like Mass-Neotek, Hosaka, and Ono-Sendai, as well as quasi-aristocratic high-orbit clans like Tessier-Ashpool, become amorphous and megalithic protagonists who divide, multiply, and operate across national boundaries, "entirely independent of the human beings who composed the body corporate" (*MLO* chap. 19). Megacompanies are more powerful than the people who compose them, more powerful than mere governments or armies. "The zaibatsus, the multinationals that shaped the course of human history, had transcended old barriers," the narrator of *Neuromancer* explains. "Viewed as organisms, they had attained a kind of immortality. You couldn't kill a zaibatsu by assassinating a dozen key executives." Suggestive of the wasp nest that Case tries to destroy, the multinationals are "hives with cybernetic memories, vast single organisms, their DNA coded in silicon" (chap. 17). Since no one person is in control of a multinational, anxiety surfaces; without knowing where authority is, an individual can't attack it effectively, and thus he or she feels defenseless.

Domination by multinationals is a manifestation of Gibson's sense that conventional reality is extremely unstable. The Other is always waiting at the periphery of one's vision, ready to invade the Self. In "The Gernsback Continuum," the narrator suffers from what his friend calls "a semiotic ghost": the American future predicted in the 1930's, complete with Art Deco gas stations and pencil sharpeners looking "as though they'd been put together wind tunnels," suddenly begins appearing in the 1980's. American culture's imagination of a future that never happened infiltrates contemporary America. Gibson thereby raises a series of ontological and epistemological questions designed to dislocate and destabilize everyday perceptions of being and knowing.

More frequent than the invasion of one world by another is the invasion of one body or mind by another. This underscores the fact that not only one's external, but even one's internal environment is unstable. An alien fuses with Coretti at the end of "The Belonging Kind." Armitage bonds fifteen toxin sacs containing mycotoxin to the lining of Case's main arteries in *Neuromancer.* Case accesses Molly's perceptions and enters her mind by means of the machine Finn sets up. Nance's parents in "Dogfight" have placed a chastity brainlock on her so she can't stand being touched by others, while Johnny Mnemonic's clients have inserted hundreds of megabytes of information he can't access into his head.

Gibson thereby interrogates the notion of selfhood, asking what exactly constitutes an individual and what it means to be human. He also interrogates the notion of the real. In a postmodern culture of simulacra, of the artificial (false eyes, limbs, and identities pervade Gibson's fiction), is there such a thing as authenticity, or is the only "reality" that which can be bought? Marly realizes that the "*real* becomes merely another concept" (*CZ* chap. 31), and Lucas that "things are seldom what they seem" (*CZ* chap. 19). Mona appears to be Angie, Armitage is really Corto, Virek has a number of different manifestations but in fact is no more than a chaos of cells kept alive in a support vat in Stockholm.

Animate and inanimate weld in Gibson's fiction. From a humanist's point of view (e.g., Kurt Vonnegut's), the human becomes less than human. From a posthumanist's point of view (e.g., Bruce Sterling's), the human becomes more than human. Humanity and machine coalesce in an act of immachination that carries many echoes, from Pynchon's SHOCK and SHROUD in *V.* (1963), to the fusion of man and rocket in *Gravity's Rainbow* (1973). Technology moves from the external to the internal, literally becoming part of us. The Yakuza assassin in "Johnny Mnemonic" possesses a jacked-up nervous system and a false thumb into which a weapon has been inserted. Lise in "The Winter Market" lives inside an artificial exoskeleton. Jack in "Burning Chrome" and Ratz in *Neuromancer* wear prosthetic arms. But if the human has become part machine, it has also become part animal. Dog, a gang member of the Lo Teks in "Johnny Mnemonic," has had a toothbud transplant from a doberman, while the cab driver in "Fragments of a Hologram Rose" looks like an ant, and Molly in *Neuromancer* regards Case with an "insect calm" (chap. 2). This recalls a prevalent theme in nineteenth-century science fiction: "the brilliance of the scientific mind is set beside a seemingly correspondent degradation of the body."[60] The ugliness of "the meat, the flesh cowboys mocked" (*N* chap. 20), contrasts violently with the essential purity of cyberspace.

If, on the one hand, the human continually merges with machine and animal, then, on the other, the human continually loses aspects of itself. Characters in Gibson's fiction lose limbs, emotions, and recollections, and replace them with a quiet yearning for what they have lost. Emblematic is Slick in *Mona Lisa Overdrive*, who spent time in a chemopenal unit and now when placed under stress can muster consecutive memory for only five minutes at a stretch. His life becomes a series of strobed moments that lead nowhere.

His personality, like so many others in Gibson's fiction, is defined by what it lacks.

Yet, perhaps contrary to some readers' expectations, many of the characters who frequent this postmodern pluriverse evince a powerful urge for survival. They refuse to capitulate in the face of a terrifying contemporary reality where change of place, personality, or physical attributes is as easy as entering a fast machine, taking a drug, or visiting a cosmetic surgeon. They become Brunneresque shockwave riders, able to undergo gratuitous and severe environmental, psychological, and physiological transformations without burning out. Like Pynchon's Tyrone Slothrop, Gibson's characters are highly suspicious of closed systems, stasis, and certainty. They are wary of conventional modes and mores. For them, normalcy equals danger. The "perfect couple" in "The Belonging Kind," for instance, turns out to be part of a pack of reptilian creatures, while the "perfect couple" in "The Gernsback Continuum" turn out to be Nazis.

DATA RUSTLERS, REPTILIAN BRAINS, AND OTHER VISIONARIES

Gibson's characters have come under fire in several ways. Some critics argue that they are secondary to stylistic pyrotechnics, others that they are simply disagreeable. Gregory Benford writes that "Gibson has labored mightily on his style and uses it to carry scenes which could have worked better if he had a better understanding of both character and situation."[61] Frederick Pohl adds that "I have yet to find a character in any cyberpunk story that I can care about or indeed believe."[62] Brian Aldiss claims that what makes *Neuromancer* "a remarkable debut, rather than a remarkable novel, is Gibson's style." Gibson's protagonist, he continues, "lacks those qualities of character we need to engage us wholly in his fate, and surface colourings, however beautifully achieved, can only titillate, not satisfy."[63]

But such assertions fail to take Gibson's work on its own terms. Moreover, they display an ignorance both of postmodern characterization and literary-historical context. By this point in time it has become a commonplace to observe that postmodern fiction (and much science fiction as well) often subverts the idea of fully-rounded character by presenting entities that are flat, insubstantial, and unstable. One need only think of Barthelme's cartoonish Snow White, Beckett's virtually nonexistent Unnamable, or Pynchon's self-deconstructive Slothrop. The intent behind adopting a narrative strategy that questions traditional characterization is to challenge traditional notions of selfhood and being by asking: what is "uniqueness"? what is "person"? what is a distinction among "selves"? what is "individual consciousness"? and what is "free will"?

Futhermore, Gibson's characters grow out of a literary tradition that tracks back at least as far as Natty Bumppo in American fiction. Speaking of James Fenimore Cooper's five Leatherstocking novels, D. H. Lawrence concludes by describing the archetypal American: "The essential American soul," he claims, "is hard, isolate, stoic, and a killer."[64] A cultural stereotype, to be sure, but one that has been admired and appropriated by Melville, Thoreau, Faulkner, Hemingway, Hammett, Chandler, *film noir*, and, of course, Gibson himself. Behind this stereotype rests two others, the American frontier and the American cowboy, with their connotations of freedom, ruggedness, discovery, and solitude. Gibson gives us a new frontier in the cyberspace matrix and the quintessential American cowboy in a series of data rustlers called "computer cowboys."

Most of his characters — and his cast is always large — are tough, high-tech lowlifes who exist at the fringes of society, in a punk or criminal culture. They are outsiders, hustlers, anarchists, black marketeers, assassins. Like Deke, a drifter in "Dogfight," who cheats at a hyped-up video game to rob a handicapped vet of money and prestige, they are out for themselves rather than for any ideology. They want credit, not political change. Many, as George Slusser points out, function at the level of the Reptilian-Complex or R-Complex, the evolutionarily most ancient part of the forebrain that, as Paul D. MacLean has shown, "plays an important role in aggressive behavior, territoriality, ritual and the establishment of social hierarchies."[65] Devouring experience in the form of new drugs, new programs and new simstims, they feel old at twenty-eight and are often scarred mentally and physically. An example is Molly. Her boyfriend has been brutally murdered, and she wears a scar that runs from just below her left nipple to the waistband of her jeans; external hurt forms an objective correlative for internal.

Although Molly has sex with Case in *Neuromancer*, Turner with Allison in *Count Zero*, and Mona with Eddy in *Mona Lisa Overdrive*, most of Gibson's characters prefer to make love to their machines rather than to each other. "I saw you stroking that Sendai," Molly tells Case. "Man, it was pornographic" (*N* chap. 3). Deke falls in love with his Spads and Fokkers game. Mona meets a man named Michael at a bar, and they go back to his place; before having sex, he sets her up in simstim recording gear so that when she is gone he can play back the episode for his own pleasure: "With the gear he had," Mona thinks, "he didn't really need anybody there" (*MLO* chap. 15). Again, Gibson provides an image of the animate and the inanimate fusing, suggesting here that sex is technology and technology sex, but he also underscores the isolation and pathos of dehumanization in a futureworld that is a metaphor for the present. When asked if people would have sex neuroelectronically if they could, Gibson answers: "Absolutely. People are almost trying to do it over the phone today. Phone sex didn't exist a couple of years ago, really, and it strikes me as horribly sad. They're going great guns."[66] In such a universe, egocentricism is rendered virtually complete. Characters are self-absorbed, sharing the assumption that private reality dominates public. They are routinely seclusive, disinterested in their surroundings except to the extent that those surroundings affect them, disturbed in their emotional responses. In other words, they exhibit a mild sort of autism.

If many of Gibson's characters have roots in the archetype of the American cowboy, then, many also have roots in the archetype of the European romantic artist. This figure tracks back at least as far as Goethe's Werther and the Byronic hero; it takes the form of an isolated, self-reliant, gloomy, questing, visionary rebel. While as much a stereotype as the cowboy, it too has been admired and appropriated by many, including Brontë, Melville, Pushkin, Nietzsche, and Kesey. Bobby Newmark --whose body decays while his mind exists solely in the infinite magical world of the aleph-- and Gentry-- a crazed prophet searching for the unifying Shape-- are only two fictional manifestations of this figure in Gibson's work, but Gibson also makes mention of real modern romantic artists like Dali, Kandinsky, Pollock, Ernst, and Cornell, as well as proto-romantic artists like Leonardo and Piranesi. Each in his own way is a visionary. Several (Dali, Ernst, Cornell) share sensibilities with Dada. Several (Kandinsky, Pollock, Piranesi) harmonize with expressionism. All except, perhaps, Leonardo embrace a surreal imagination which asserts, along with André Breton, that "the real process of thought" lies in "the omnipotence of dream," that "the poet must turn *seer*," and that "it is time to have done with the provoking insanities of 'realism.'"[67] Riviera in *Neuromancer* embodies this type. A walking surrealist painting, he possesses implants that project holograms of what he imagines onto reality, be it a giant human spermatozoon swimming in Case's Bourbon and water or a trout darting out of a man's mouth. Of course, the cyberspace matrix itself becomes a surrealist offering in this context as well. Yet art in Gibson's universe is not simply a liberating visionary expression. It is also, as Virek and Marly well know, a lucrative if dangerous business too.

Looking for a moment at several of the artist figures that appear in Gibson's work, one can begin to piece together Gibson's sense of the artist's role in society. The artist, like Lise in "The Winter Market" and computer cowboys such as Case in

Neuromancer, probes the unknown, the Jungian depths of the unconscious, and brings back something he or she then shapes into story, sound, or form. True artists, the narrator of "The Winter Market" knows, "are able to break the surface tension, dive down deep, down and out, out into Jung's sea, and bring back — well, dreams." These dreams are then "structured, balanced, turned into art." Moreover the artist, like Angie the simstim queen in *Mona Lisa Overdrive*, allows the world to live through his or her heightened sensations. Traditional notions of realism do not play into this, as Sandii in "New Rose Hotel" understands; she writes and rights her past, making her history into fiction. Usually the act of creation doesn't occur, however, without taking its toll. While Slick Henry finds a certain amount of "pleasure" in building the Judge, in getting the Judge "out where [Slick] could see him and keep track of him and finally, sort of, be free of the idea of him," he admits he ultimately hates his creation (*MLO* chap. 10). Usually the artist is self-destructive (Mona, Angie), or diseased (Lise, Bobby).

When Molly passes through Tessier-Ashpool's library and gallery in their high-orbit space station, she notices "a shattered, dust-stenciled sheet of glass" below which is a brass plaque that reads: *"La mariée mise à nu par ses célibataires, même"* (N chap. 17). This identifies the work as Duchamp's assemblage, "The Bride Stripped Bare by Her Bachelors, Even." Whereas the collage is a modernist technique developed by Picasso and Braque during their Cubist phase and typically involves adding fragments of newspaper or other printed matter to one's composition, the assemblage is a postmodernist technique developed by the Dadaists and celebrated by the Dadaist revival of the 1950's by creators like Rauschenberg, Cornell, and (in literature) Burroughs, and it typically involves adding three-dimensional found material to one's composition. The result of the assemblage is commonly the creation of spatial disharmony and incongruity that often evinces itself in readerly or viewerly disorientation. Art, then, becomes bricolage — literally a collection of garbage — and bricoleurs frequent Gibson's work. One thinks of the manipulator that makes quasi-Cornell boxes in *Count Zero* and, of course, Slick Henry in *Mona Lisa Overdrive*. Rubin, Slick's literary cousin who appears in "The Winter Market," calls himself a *gomi no sensei*, Japanese for *a master of junk*. "What he's the master of, really," the reader is told, "is garbage, kipple, refuse, the sea of cast-off goods our century floats on."

Gibson makes the same claim for himself: "I see myself as a kind of literary collage-artist [though perhaps assemblage-artist would be more appropriate here], and sf as a marketing framework that allows me to gleefully ransack the whole fat supermarket of 20th century cultural symbols."[68] The artists in his work are manifestations of Gibson-as-artist. He looks around himself and gathers together a massive amount of cultural material from the last part of the twentieth century as though it were so much waste. He builds from the detritus of contemporary culture. By doing so, he implies that contemporary culture is simply so much detritus, garbage, a heterogeneous mixture of leftovers from the pop hypermart, literature, film, history, science, and so on. He embraces postmodern polyphony, adores the idea of undifferentiation, and becomes — like so many of his characters following in the tradition of Burroughs, Barthelme, and Pynchon — a visionary *gomi no sensei*.

PYROTECHNICS AND THE READERLY CRISIS

"This process of cultural mongrelization seems to be what postmodernism is all about," Gibson affirms. "The result is a generation of people (some of whom are artists) whose tastes are wildly eclectic — the kind of people who are hip to punk music and Mozart, who seem to rent these terrible horror and SF movies from the 7-Eleven most nights but who will occasionally call you up to go see mud wrestling or a poetry reading."[69] Ideas of compartmentalization and hierarchism crumble in the postmodern imagination. The effect for many readers is liberating. For others, whose imaginations are shaped by a modernist education based on laws of canonization that presuppose a distinction between "high" and "low" culture, between "good" and "bad" art, the effect is threatening. It problematizes the very foundations of conventional aesthetic judgment. Postmodern writing, for better or worse, becomes Einsteinian network rather than Newtonian monolith. It becomes, as Roland Barthes suggests, "a tissue of quotations drawn from the innumerable centres of culture."[70]

It is not difficult to see this in Gibson's project on a generic level. Most often considered a science-fiction writer, Gibson employs various extrapolations of technology or pseudo-technology. But he also appropriates stylized cowboys, scouts, and bad guys, the adventurous frontier mentality, and motifs of the shootout and bar-room brawl from the western. From the spy thriller, which portrays a Pynchonesque vision of contemporary reality, he borrows convoluted plot, ideas of international conspiracy, and vast bewildering political or corporate powers, secret agents, and evil henchmen. He lifts lowlife sleuths and criminals, archetypal tough guys, mysteries solved through the collection and interpretation of clues, seedy underworld settings, clipped prose, and sparse dialogue from the hard-boiled detective genre. He adopts a sense of pervasive magic, horror, and ghosts, long underground passageways, and dark staircases from the gothic novel-- and formal distortions, bizarre characters, decadent settings, absurd incongruity, and a fascination with the irrational and abnormal from the Southern grotesque tradition. From the tradition of the *Erziehungsroman*, he takes the plot of education that traces the psychological journey of a youth from innocence to experience, like Bobby in *Count Zero* and Kumiko in *Mona Lisa Overdrive*.

Writing-as-network also evinces itself in individual passages. The following, which occurs at the outset of *Neuromancer*, is indicative of Gibson's fiction and may serve as an introduction to how to read Gibson closely. Here, Case returns to his sleeping compartment from a hard day only to meet Molly for the first time:

Fluorescents came on as he crawled in.

"Close the hatch real slow, friend. You still got that Saturday night special you rented from the waiter?"

She sat with her back to the wall, at the far end of the coffin. She had her knees up, resting her wrists on them; the pepperbox muzzle of a flechette pistol emerged from her hands. . . . She wore mirrored glasses. Her clothes were black, the heels of black boots deep in the temperfoam. . . . She shook her head. He realized the glasses were surgically inset, sealing her sockets. The silver lenses seemed to grow from smooth pale skin above her cheekbones, framed by dark hair cut in a rough shag. The fingers curled around the fletcher were slender, white, tipped with polished burgundy. The nails looked artificial. . .

. "So what do you want, lady?" He sagged back against the hatch.

"You. One live body, brains still somewhat intact. Molly, Case. My name's Molly. I'm collecting you for the man I work for. Just wants to talk, is all. Nobody wants to hurt you."

"That's good."

"'Cept I do hurt people sometimes, Case. I guess it's just the way I'm wired." She wore tight black gloveleather jeans and a bulky black jacket cut from some matte fabric that seemed to absorb light . . . . The fletcher vanished into the black jacket . . . . "You try to fuck around with me, you'll be taking one of the stupidest chances of your whole life."

She held out her hands, palms up, the white fingers slightly spread, and with a barely audible click, ten double-edged, four-centimeter scalpel blades slid from their housings beneath the burgundy nails.

She smiled. The blades slowly withdrew. (*N* chap. 1)

As Paul Alkon astutely comments, emphasis falls not on scientific detail but on the marvelous. Unlike much science fiction that depends on gadgetry for its effects, Gibson's work usually focuses on the magic inherent in a situation. Here the scene partakes of motifs associated to a large extent with "pulp fiction transformed to a futuristic setting with some appropriate changes of costume, decor and vocabulary" — until, that is, Molly reveals the scalpel blades inset in her fingertips.[71] Suddenly, the world tilts. Molly becomes, not a tough-gal from a hard-boiled detective novel, but a sorceress. The universe of technology slips since "it is very hard to understand how a four-centimeter (1.6 inch) retractable blade along with even a highly miniaturized motor-mechanism could be implanted without impeding ability to bend the fingers at their first joints, although some ingenious explanation could doubtless be offered."[72] By refusing to explain the technology behind this scene, Gibson as usual underscores the scene's astonishing aspects, thereby taking it out of the realm of science fiction and placing it firmly in the realm of the marvelous. Much the same happens to the cyberspace matrix when Gibson introduces voodoo gods into it. Like Tzvetan Todorov's fantastic, Gibson's work tends to keep two possibilities open at once: with this scene, technology/magic; with the cyberspace matrix, technology/religion. Perhaps employing such a strategy helps account for Brin's assertion that Gibson, along with other cyberpunks, "prefer[s] to craft 'scientist' characters who behave exactly like the magicians and wizards of fantasy."[73]

This strategy is also another case of writing-as-network. In a single passage, Gibson not only brings together the universes of fantasy and science fiction, but also those of the detective novel (the dingy setting, clipped prose, and tough-guy dialogue), the western (Molly's boots, gun, and black clothes suggest the archetypal evil cowboy), the spy thriller (Molly, part secret agent and part lowlife henchwoman, introduces the conspiracy plot here), and the realist novel (the description of the sleeping compartment is an accurate one of Japan's current low-cost, business hotel rooms). Little wonder, therefore, that a sense of the artificial pervades this scene from the fluorescent lights to the fact that Molly is literally "wired" differently from most humans. Like Molly, who is an amalgamation of technology and humanity, the text itself is an amalgamation of various narrative modes. By mongrelizing discursive worlds, Gibson mongrelizes the beliefs about existence those discursive worlds suggest. Compartmentalization and hierarchism gone, each discursive world becomes simply one of many, relatively as good or bad as any other. Thus devalued, each discursive world becomes one more instance of *gomi*, refusing humanist ideas of totality, absolute significance, and closure.

Rirdan faults Gibson's prose style on a number of grounds, including the fact that it both is "ambiguous" and embraces "mystification for the sake of mystification."[74] But, given the preceding, it is clear that ambiguity and mystification are exactly what Gibson is after. In a characteristic move, Gibson "mystifies" the above scene from the start by giving the reader dialogue without accompanying tags: Molly speaks without the reader knowing it is she who is speaking; then, she is described; but through a narrative slight-of-hand, she isn't named until nearly two-thirds of the way through the passage. In addition, again characteristically, futurist concepts and devices like the "coffin" and "flechette pistol" are cited long before they have been explained, so that the reader has the impression he or she has missed the explanation. Frequently one must glean meaning from context (as with the word "coffin" here), and sometimes one must wait pages for illumination (as with the word "ghost" in the first sentence of *Mona Lisa Overdrive*). The effect is close to that of the cinematic jump cut found in MTV videos that produces discontinuity in filmic time while drawing attention to the medium itself. It is as though, as Donald Barthelme has claimed in another context, that, just as modern painters had to reinvent painting because of the discovery of photography, so contemporary writers have had to reinvent writing because of the discovery of film."[75]

The reader is further disoriented by the Pynchonesque premium Gibson's style places on poetic information density. Gibson is infatuated with detail and inventory, from the pepperbox muzzle of the flechette pistol to Molly's heels sinking into the temperfoam, from Molly's hairstyle to the color of her fingernails. This infatuation is foreign to most science fiction, and much conventional fiction as well. Gibson regularly loads his sentences with a blend of high-tech jargon, brand names, street slang, and acronyms that lends an overall sense of urgency, intensity and at times congestion to his style. He commonly uses prose as others might use poetry. Words like "cyberspace" and "black matte" are repeated with the incantational power of figurative language. A title like "Burning Chrome" functions initially at a purely metaphorical and oxymoronic level with its connotations of heat, rage, desire, animation, and life on the one hand, and of coolness, sleakness, dispassion, inanimation, and technology on the other; only well into the story by that name does the reader discover that "burning" means "sabotaging a computer system" and that "Chrome" is a woman's name.

Gibson utilizes colors with a similar poetic intensity. In the above passage, as in much of Gibson's fiction, black and white dominate and tend to occur in succession. Molly's jacket, jeans, boots, and presumably hair are black and seem "to absorb light," just as Molly is in the process of "absorbing" Case and his freedom into a deadly conspiracy. Her cheekbones and fingers are white; rather than traditional associations of innocence and purity, though, this color in Gibson's work carries associations with the pale skin worn by the living dead like the Draculas in *Mona Lisa Overdrive* who possess "bone-thin, bone-white faces" (chap. 32). Gray, the color that appears with the next greatest frequency in Gibson's fiction and that is negatively associated with such things as Mona's "suits" (or johns), the dead earth, and the aleph, is absent in this passage, but its metallic double, silver, appears in Molly's mirrorshades and, apparently, her scalpel blades. Silver is ordinarily associated with the technological in Gibson, as is its near cousin, chrome. Black, white and silver coalesce here in a visual pun that transforms Molly into a *femme fatale*, a "catty" woman who is half-animal, half-machine.

Three significant metaphors occur in the passage: 1) the lenses of Molly's mirrorshades seem to "grow" from the skin above her cheekbones; 2) Molly acts violently because she is "wired" that way; 3) her clothes seem to "absorb light." This again is indicative of Gibson's poetic prose. While a number of rather conventional metaphors occur in Gibson's fiction, simply linking attributes of two objects from some generally similar category, the most interesting ones often link something natural with something artificial. Mirrorshades "grow" like plants out of Molly's skin. Molly's behavior is "wired" like a machine. Her clothes "absorb light" like a black hole. Or, elsewhere in *Neuromancer*, the sky is "the color of television, turned to a dead channel" (chap. 1), a silk scarf is patterned like microcircuits (chap. 1), and young men and women hang-gliding are "machines built for racing" (chap. 10). If the romantic metaphor makes nature familiar and technology unfamiliar, these postmodern metaphors make nature unfamiliar and technology familiar. As Richard Kearney asserts concerning the postmodern imagination in general: "The contemporary eye is no longer innocent. What we see is almost invariably informed by prefabricated images. There is, of course, a fundamental difference between the image of today and of former times: now the image *precedes* the reality it is supposed to represent."[76]

Such metaphors partake in the aesthetics of the unpleasant, which has its roots in the poetry of Eliot in the twentieth century, Baudelaire in the nineteenth. For Gibson, a road is "dead straight, like a neat incision, laying the city open" (*N* chap. 7). Turner's hands are "distant creatures, pale undersea things that lived a life of their own far down at the bottom of some unthinkable Pacific trench" (*CZ* chap. 14). The plot of a soap opera is "a multiheaded narrative tapeworm that coiled back in to devour itself every few months, then sprouted new heads hungry for tension and thrust" (*CZ* chap. 9). Given such astonishing use of language, it may easily be argued that Gibson's focus is not on conventional plot at all, but on accumulation of detail and turns of phrase. Gibson's fiction is less about what happens, or to whom, or where, than it is about style. Like Molly herself in the above passage, Gibson's is a fiction of artifice. In this way, Gibson (as he says) is "definitely of the termite school" in that he tends to zero in on "the little corners of things more than the way the whole thing looks."[77]

Gibson adopts the idea of the "termite school" from a 1962 essay by the iconoclastic film critic Manny Farber. Farber distinguishes between two kinds of art. The first, for which he holds nothing but contempt, is White Elephant Art. This is the art that embraces the idea of "well-regulated area, both logical and magical," embodied by the films of François Truffaut. Proponents of this neoclassical "school" produce tedious pieces that are "ungiving and puzzling," "clogging weight-density-structure-polish amalgam[s] associated with self-aggrandizing masterwork[s]," reminiscent of Rube Goldberg's perpetual-motion machines. The second kind of art, which Farber advocates, is Termite Art. This is the art that stands opposed to "gilt culture," embracing freedom and multiplicity, embodied by the films of Laurel and Hardy. Proponents of this neoromantic "school" produce pieces that go "always forward eating [their] own boundaries, and, likely as not, leave nothing in [their] path other than the signs of eager, industrious, unkempt activity." A kind of postmodernism, Termite Art has no goal except to devour its own boundaries, fuse genres, and create a space "where the spotlight of culture is nowhere in evidence, so that the craftsman can be ornery, wasteful, stubbornly self-involved, doing go-for-broke art and not caring what comes of it."[78]

Often Gibson's emphasis on writing-as-network, ambiguity, mystification for mystification's sake, information density, obsession with detail, highly metaphoric prose, and the aesthetics of the unpleasant adds up to a sense of confusion and uneasiness on the reader's part. Dropped without much exposition into an alien and sometimes obscure futureworld, the reader is put in the uncomfortable position of having to make decisions about meaning and moral value based on very little textual evidence. If trained as a modernist, ready to search for patterns of intelligibility, the reader experiences an analogue of what John Brunner calls "overload" and Ted Mooney "information sickness," a radical disorientation before a plethora of facts that might or might not connect. All fiction is at least in part a kind of game, essentially gratuitous, an end in itself. Play is a voluntary activity that creates order and hence "meaning" in a limited environment, and usually in play there are three kinds of players: those who play by the rules, those who cheat, and those who refuse to play. But postmodern fiction differs from other kinds of fiction both by acknowledging its existence as game in an extremely self-conscious way, and by adding a fourth kind of player to the game. This fourth player, an emblem of the reader, is one who very much wants to play but does not know the rules, and hence cannot win or even sit at the table. For a modernist reader, this is a particularly unpleasant role in which to find oneself. However for a postmodern reader, this is simply one more example of the need to be a flexible shockwave rider.

Gibson reminds us about this numerous times in the course of his fiction. At the end of *Count Zero*, Turner gives Angie a biosoft dossier and says: "It doesn't tell the whole story. Remember that. Nothing ever does" (chap. 34). The dossier, like the novel itself, supposedly holds a narrative that should make sense of things. But at the same time Gibson offers the possibility of significance and closure with one hand, he subjects the possibility to contradiction or cancellation with the other. Just as the dossier (to which neither Angie nor the reader gains access in *Count Zero*) "doesn't tell the whole story," so too the novel itself promises meaning only to defer meaning to its sequel, *Mona Lisa Overdrive*, which itself concludes, not with illumination, but with a promise that truth is just around the corner and that we'll arrive there "in a New York minute" (chap. 45) — though, ironically, *Mona Lisa Overdrive* is the last book in the Matrix Trilogy, and the only "meaning" the reader can obtain in a New York minute is to return to the beginning of the Trilogy and start reading again in an endless cycle. The story almost makes sense, but not quite. The almost-making-sense seems to indicate meaning has only been deferred temporarily. But that is not the case. Meaning, it slowly dawns on the reader, is contained in the failure to achieve meaning.

Perhaps the best advice to the modernist reader, fraught with frustration, disorientation, and the perpetually nagging feeling he or she has just missed something in Gibson's fiction, comes from Slick Henry in *Mona Lisa Overdrive*. At one point Gentry, the mainframe mystic obsessed with the metaphysics of cyberspace, launches into a complex "explanation" of the aleph into which Bobby is plugged. "As always," the narrator says, speaking from Slick's point of view, "once Gentry got going, he used words and constructions that Slick had trouble understanding, but Slick knew from experience that it was easier not to interrupt him; the trick was in pulling some kind of meaning out of the overall flow, skipping over the parts you didn't understand" (chap. 21). It is a mistake to read Gibson with a Pynchonesque paranoid abandon, trying to connect everything with everything; the result will be a modernist's anger and anxiety. Often things will not connect, and ultimately Gibson intends to leave a number of large and small questions unanswered. It is impossible, for example, to know whether the United States still exists as a political entity in the Matrix Trilogy, even though much of the action apparently takes place in them, and it is impossible to locate Dog Solitude in the Trilogy's geography. It is as fruitless to ask whether Gibson embraces or eschews technology as it is to ask how those four-centimeter retractable blades could fit in Molly's fingers or what precisely those voodoo gods are that seem to inhabit the matrix. Rather than worrying about words and constructions one has trouble understanding, the reader is best off keeping in mind that Gibson is deliberately giving him or her trouble in order to raise fundamental questions about the nature of meaning, humanity's need to make cosmos out of chaos, and humanity's increasing inability to do so as it moves into a new millennium. The "trick" to reading Gibson is to pull some kind of meaning out of the overall flow, skip over the parts one doesn't understand, and delight in Gibson's dazzlingly imaginative pyrotechnics at the level of scene and sentence. And, most of all, enjoy the shockwave.

Endnotes

[1] "I just loved *Neuromancer* and couldn't resist," Acker wrote me in a letter dated June, 1989. "I wrote Bill Gibson my first fan letter ever and told him I was plagiarizing his work. He wrote back, I can't quote exactly, — we don't call it 'plagiarism,' dear, but 'appropriation.'"
[2] Thomas M. Disch, "Mona Lisa Overdrive," *New York Times Book Review* 11 December 1988, 23.
[3] Istvan Csicsery-Ronay, "Cyberspace," *American Book Review* 10.6 (January-February 1989), 7.
[4] Larry McCaffery, "An Interview with William Gibson," *Mississippi Review* 16.2 & 3 (1988), 223, 224, 233.
[5] See Danny Rirdan, "The Works of William Gibson," *Foundation* 43 (Summer 1988), 36-46. Gibson disagrees with Rirdan, arguing that this simply implies massive data-flow, and is consistent with extrapolation.
[6] Gibson again takes exception, pointing out that such pills actually exist.
[7] McCaffery, 233.
[8] From a letter to me dated July, 1989.
[9] Joseph Nicholas and Judith Hanna, "William Gibson," *Interzone* 1.13 (1985), 18.
[10] Marian MacNair, "Mainframe Voodoo," *Montreal Mirror* 7-20 April, 1989, 23.
[11] Leanne C. Harper, "The Culture of Cyberspace," *The Bloomsbury Review* 8.5 (September/October 1988), 16.
[12] Victoria Hamburg, "The King of Cyberspace," *Interview* January 1989, 86.
[13] Candas Jane Dorsey, "Beyond Cyberspace," *Books in Canada* June-July 1988, 12.
[14] Bruce Sterling, "Preface," *Mirrorshades: The Cyberpunk Anthology* (New York: Arbor House, 1986), xii.
[15] Alvin Toffler, *The Third Wave* (New York: William Morrow, 1980), 325.
[16] Kevin Kelly, "Cyberpunk Era," *Whole Earth Review* Summer: 1989, 80.
[17] McCaffery, 226. But now Gibson feels this is an overstatement that needs to be toned down.
[18] Carol McGuirk, "The 'New' Romancers: Science Fiction Innovators from Gernsback to Gibson," paper delivered at the Fiction 2000 conference at the University of Leeds, June 28-July 1, 1989.
[19] Although Gibson told me he has not seen *Tron* yet.
[20] Nicholas and Hanna, 18.
[21] Hamburg, 86.
[22] From a letter to me dated July, 1989.
[23] Tom Maddox, "Cobra, She Said: An Interim Report on the Fiction of William Gibson," *Fantasy Review* 9.4 (April 1986), 46.
[24] Fredric Jameson [with Anders Stephanson], "Regarding Postmodernism — A Conversation with Fredric Jameson," in *Universal Abandon? The Politics of Postmodernism* (Minneapolis: U Minnesota P, 1988), 18.

25 Hamburg, 86.
26 Darko Suvin, *Metamorphoses of Science Fiction: On the Poetics and History of a Literary Genre* (New Haven: Yale UP, 1979), 4.
27 Nicholas and Hanna, 18.
28 MacNair, 23.
29 McCaffery, 230.
30 Harper, 30.
31 Harper, 16.
32 Istvan Csicsery-Ronay, "Cyberpunk and Neuromanticism," *Mississippi Review* 16.2 & 3 (1988), 269.
33 Sterling, ix
34 Anonymous editorial, "Requiem for the Cyberpunks," *Science Fiction Eye* 1.1 (Winter 1987): 5.
35 Sterling, x.
36 Ibid., xii.
37 Ibid., xiii.
38 Ibid., xiii.
39 Ibid, xi.
40 F. T. Marinetti, "The Joy of Mechanical Force," in *The Modern Tradition*, ed. Richard Ellmann and Charles Feidelson, Jr. (New York: Oxford UP, 1965), 433.
41 Gibson took several courses as an undergraduate at UBC, but says he didn't learn anything from them. His interest in art history, he claims, is "fetishistic." He obsesses on a given artist, learning all he can about him or her. His knowledge of art history is nowhere more apparent than in *CZ*.
42 Gregory Benford, "Is Something Going On?" *Mississippi Review* 16.2 & 3 (1988), 22.
43 David Brin, "Starchilde Harold, Revisited," *Mississippi Review* 16.2 & 3 (1988), 26.
44 Csicsery-Ronay, "Cyberpunk and Neuromanticism," 268.
45 Larry McCaffery, "The Cyberpunk Controversy," *Mississippi Review* 16.2 & 3 (1988), 9.
46 In fact, Gibson hasn't read *The Third Wave*, although he was clearly exposed to many of its ideas through the Sterling and Shiner connections.
47 Toffler, 289.
48 Ibid., 357.
49 Csicsery-Ronay, "Cyberpunk and Neuromanticism," 266.
50 See Jean-François Lyotard, *The Postmodern Condition*, trans. Geoff Bennington and Brian Massumi (Minneapolis: U Minnesota P, 1984); Allen Thiher, *Words in Reflection: Modern Language Theory and Postmodern Fiction* (Chicago: Chicago UP, 1984); Charles Caramello, *Silverless Mirrors: Book, Self and Postmodern American Fiction* (Tallahassee: UP Florida, 1983); Brian McHale, *Postmodernist Fiction* (New York:

Methuen, 1987); Jean Baudrillard, "The Ecstasy of Communication," trans. John Johnston, in *The Anti-Aesthetic: Essays on Postmodern Culture*, ed. Hal Foster (Port Townsend: Bay Press, 1983): 126-133; Andreas Huyssen, *After the Great Divide: Modernism, Mass Culture, Postmodernism* (Bloomington: Indiana UP, 1986).

[51] See Gianni Vattimo, *The End of Modernity: Nihilism and Hermeneutics in Postmodern Culture*, trans. Jon R. Snyder (Baltimore: Johns Hopkins UP, 1988).

[52] Toffler, 361.

[53] See Alan Wilde, *Horizons of Assent: Modernism, Postmodernism, and the Ironic Imagination* (Baltimore: John's Hopkins UP, 1981); John Brunner, *The Shockwave Rider* (New York: Ballantine, 1975), 53; and Linda Hutcheon, *A Poetics of Postmodernism: History, Theory, and Fiction* (New York: Routledge, 1988).

[54] McHale, 65-72.

[55] Hamburg, 84.

[56] Grania Davis, "Foreword," in *The Best Japanese Science Fiction Stories*, ed. John L. Apostolou and Martin H. Greenberg (New York: Dembner Books, 1989), 12.

[57] McCaffery, "Interview," 226.

[58] Hamburg, 86.

[59] Ibid., 86.

[60] C. N. Manlove, *Science Fiction: Ten Explorations* (Ohio: Kent State UP, 1986), 5.

[61] Benford, 20.

[62] Frederick Pohl, untitled essay, *Mississippi Review* 16.2 & 3 (1988), 46.

[63] Brian Aldiss, *Trillion Year Spree: The History of Science Fiction* (London: Victor Gallancz, 1986), 412-13.

[64] D. H. Lawrence, "Fenimore Cooper's Leatherstocking Novels," in *Studies in Classic American Literature* (New York: Doubleday, 1953), 73.

[65] Carl Sagan discusses Paul D. MacLean in *The Dragons of Eden: Speculations on the Evolution of Human Intelligence* (New York: Random House, 1977), 60. George Slusser's paper on the R-Complex and cyberpunk was delivered at the Fiction 2000 conference at the University of Leeds, June 28-July 1, 1989. See, too, Tom Maddox's story, "Snake-Eyes," which enacts the image, *Mirrorshades: The Cyberpunk Anthology*, ed. Bruce Sterling (New York: Arbor House, 1986), 13-34.

[66] Hamburg, 84.

[67] André Breton, "Surrealism," in *The Modern Tradition*, ed. Richard Ellmann and Charles Feidelson, Jr. (New York: Oxford UP, 1965), 602, 605, 613.

[68] Nicholas and Hanna, 17.

[69] McCaffery, "Interview," 220.

[70] Roland Barthes, "The Death of the Author," in *Image Music Text*, trans. Stephen Heath (New York: Hill and Wang, 1977), 146.

[71] Paul Alkon, "Deus Ex Machina in William Gibson's Cyberpunk Trilogy,"

paper delivered at the Fiction 2000 conference at the University of Leeds, June 28-July 1, 1989, 6-7.

[72] Alkon, 8.

[73] Brin, 25.

[74] Rirdan, 44.

[75] Donald Barthelme, "Symposium on Fiction," *Shenandoah* 27.2 (1976), 3-31.

[76] Richard Kearny, *The Wake of the Imagination* (Minneapolis: U Minnesota P, 1988), 2.

[77] Takayuki Tatsumi, "An Interview with William Gibson," *Science Fiction Eye* 1.1 (Winter 1987), 7.

[78] Manny Farber, "White Elephant Art vs. Termite Art," in *Negative Space* (New York: Praeger, 1971), 134-144. Gibson read this while attending UBC, and says it is one of the few essays that directly influenced his aesthetics.

Burning Chrome

No one can change the future.
All anyone can do is try to be a part of it.
   —Lewis Shiner, *Deserted Cities of the Heart*

An illuminating place to begin making some sense of Gibson's work is *Burning Chrome* (1986), in which Gibson collects the shorter pieces he wrote and published between 1977 and 1986. Prefaced by another Sterling manifesto, these pages evince Gibson's early development as a craftsperson. Sterling argues that with these stories Gibson was instrumental in waking 1980's science fiction from "its dogmatic slumbers" by casting it "from its cave into the bright sunlight of the modern zeitgeist." Throughout the course of these pieces, Gibson moves from experimentation at the level of technique to experimentation at the level of idea, evolves the near-future geography that will become his signature, and even tries to interrogate traditional notions of authorship by collaborating on three stories with other cyberpunks. Meanwhile, he also explores a number of themes that will become central to his major work.

"Fragments of a Hologram Rose" (1977) is his first, briefest, and stylistically most innovative short fiction. He wrote it in 1976 in lieu of a final paper for a science-fiction course he took at the University of British Columbia. It was published a year later by *Unearth*, a low-circulation Boston magazine. Parker, the story's protagonist, was an indentured servant to a Japanese combine when a teenager. Now he is a thirty-year-old dream-merchant who programs proto-simstim devices called ASP (Apparent Sensory Perception) decks. Ironically, his own dream, a love-affair with a woman named Angela, has recently failed. While searching through her closet, Parker discovers an emblem of their love, a postcard of a hologram rose, which he throws down the garbage disposal. He then jacks into an ASP tape containing some of Angela's perceptions only to realize how little he has understood of her past and point-of-view. He recognizes that, suggestive of the shreds of the hologram rose, "we're each other's fragments." We are never able to see the total picture of each other, the world, or even ourselves. We must learn to live with pieces in the absence of wholes.

Gibson himself points out four key themes evident in the story "in larval form." First is "the protagonist who seems barely able to drag himself out of bed." Second is the "theme of memory, of cybernetic systems as a metaphor for the working of human memory." Third is "a sort of prefiguring of Punk." Fourth is "the sense of Big Corporations moving around in the background, and the idea of indentured servitude to the same."[1] To these, the reader should add at least two other important ones. Gibson juxtaposes the tranquil pristine dreamscape of ASP with the painful material world, thereby anticipating the mind/body dualism that will eventually take the form of cyberspace/reality. Furthermore, the reader learns for the first time that human beings make love with their machines because they cannot make love to other human beings.

Still more interesting is Gibson's early experimentation with narrative technique. Like the hologram rose of the title, this story is fragmented into small sections. It is a story about fragmentation: of the self, of human relationships, and even of language. Intensely poetic shards of sentence appear throughout the piece, as do such surreal images as the cabby who, dressed in respirator and goggles, looks like an ant as he drives Angela away through acid rain. Gibson occasionally switches from third- to second-person point-of-view, emphasizing the relativity of perception. He self-reflexively inserts a passage from a fictitous history of the 1990's into his narrative, refuses to spend much time fleshing out Angela's character, and withholds such traditional motivational information about Parker as why he wanted to escape from the American subsidiary of a Japanese combine. In other words, he foregrounds innovative form over traditional content, hence generating a general lack of affect both at the level of character and tone.

Nothing could be less true of "The Gernsback Continuum" (1981), which adopts a first-person point-of-view and conventional narrative strategy. This time the unnamed protagonist is a photographer, initially a believer in realism, who travels to London to shoot a series of shoe ads. Through Cohen, his boss, he meets a pop-art historian, Dialta Downes, currently at work on an illustrated history called *The Airstream Futuropolis: The Tomorrow That Never Was* about the American SF imagination of the 1930's which predicted a streamlined future that never happened. The photographer flies to the southwest to shoot 1930s architecture for Downes, only to discover that somehow he has "penetrated a fine membrane, a membrane of probability." "Semiotic ghost[s]" from this fictional future begin seeping into his world. The story culminates in a vision of a Tucson complete with crystal roads, golden temples, and gyrocopters shaped like dragonflies. In a dualistic move, Gibson keeps two possibilities open at once: either the photographer's vision is a fantastic prophecy, or it is simply a speed-induced hallucination. Gibson thereby shortcircuits the gravity of realism in which the photographer initially believed.

Gibson's plot is highly reminiscent of Jorge Luis Borges's in "Tlön, Uqbar, Orbis Tertius" (1941), in which a fantastic ideal world called Tlön gradually penetrates the real one. Both fictions depict apparently ideal imaginary worlds that, in fact, turn out to be dangerous. In the former, contact with the Tlönic universe slowly disintegrates the real one; in the latter, the Jungian "subconscious of the Thirties" carries with it "a kind of totalitarian dignity, like the stadiums Albert Speer built for Hitler." Both pieces suggest that human beings prefer artificial and potentially deadly order to the all-too-real chaos of everyday life. Both point to the inherent instability of a reality into which epistemological and ontological illegality can irrupt at any moment.

But "The Gernsback Continuum" also functions as a kind of self-reflexive gloss on the genre of which it is a part. Sterling, in his preface to *Burning Chrome*, correctly asserts that Gibson is "consciously drawing a bead on the shambling figure of the SF tradition." While technically a much more conservative fiction than "Fragments of a Hologram Rose," "The Gernsback Continuum" nonetheless is thematically a much more subversive one. Gibson employs intertextuality to sabotage the SF tradition. As McGuirk notes, the fiction's climactic scene recalls the plot of John Campbell's "Twilight" (1934) in which a superman from the future materializes in the Nevada desert.[2] Such a strategy directly challenges science-fiction's Golden Age embodied by Hugo Gernsback who began *Amazing Stories* in 1926 and whose name appears in the story's title. The future of America's past imagined reveals the past's conservative subconscious, and it is no coincidence that this past finds such a congenial home in the politically conservative 1980's. The photographer witnesses a perfect young couple materialize in the Arizona desert, a beatific vision of Tucson in the background. The couple is white, blond, and blue-eyed. They wear spotless white clothing and are "smug, happy, and utterly content in themselves and their world." They are *too* perfect, *too* clean, and *too* content. Their presence conjures "all the sinister fruitiness of Hitler Youth propaganda." Gibson thus makes the claim that the grubby and chaotic real future might well be preferable to the ideal one imagined by the mass subconscious of the 1930's.

The "perfect" couple are emblems of idealized conformity. Their danger lies in the fact that they are utterly static, unindividuated representatives of a closed system. They accordingly register Gibson's deeply Pynchonesque suspicion of normalcy, a theme which he probes again in "The Belonging Kind" (1981), another tale of invasion. Gibson recalls it began as a private joke between John Shirley and him. Shirley sent him "a very very long manuscript, and I thought it was an overly serious, and somewhat absurd piece of work," Gibson explains. "I wrote a certain parody of what he had written. He altered it a little bit and sold it."[3]

The plot of "The Belonging Kid" has more to do with horror's investigation of subconscious fear than with science-fiction's investigation of technological innovation. Michael Coretti teaches linguistics at a community college. About thirty, he lives on the fringes of society, seeing himself as "the Martian dresser, the eavesdropper, the outsider, the one whose clothes and conversation never fit." He frequents bars, where one night he meets a woman named Antoinette who interests him because she perfectly mimics the speech, walk, and appearance of others. When he follows her, he finds she literally sheds one personality and takes on another so that, chameleon-like, she can fit into any environment in which she finds herself. Like the perfect couple in "The Gernsback Continuum," she becomes "the personification of conformity." Obsessed with her, since she offers him what he has never been able to have, Coretti misses classes, loses his job, and moves into a dingy apartment. He rides home with Antoinette and her male friend one night to stumble upon a hotel room full of virtually identical reptilian creatures masquerading as humans. Over time, desperate to belong, Coretti turns into one of them.

Coretti becomes a "real human" only by sacrificing his humanity. Like the designers who created the future that never happened in "The Gernsback Continuum," Coretti is a populist "trying to give the public what it wanted." He tries so hard to do so that he becomes something less than human, appropriating the gills and tentacles of the belonging kind. Not only an indictment of normalcy, this fiction is also a statement about the radical contingency of selfhood. It considers how near the self continually is to metamorphosing into something other than self. The implication is that matters of identity, life, and death are completely beyond one's control. Insidious change is spontaneous and irresistable.

Next comes "Johnny Mnemonic" (1981), start of the Sprawl series that will also include "Burning Chrome" (1982) and "New Rose Hotel" (1984). For the first time, Gibson begins to sketch in the geography of the Matrix Trilogy. "The triumph of these pieces," as Sterling writes in his preface to *Burning Chrome*, is "their brilliant, self-consistent evocation of a credible future. It is hard to overestimate the difficulty of this effort, which is one that many SF writers have been ducking for years." "Johnny Mnemonic" marks a new kind of character, a new tone, and a new high-density style for Gibson. The paradigmatic American — hard, isolate, stoic, and a killer — surfaces. The tone fuses Gibson's earlier hip irony of Pynchon and Burroughs, with the tough-guy prose of Chandler and Hammett. The style moves toward characteristic ambiguity: dialogue tags drop out, pronoun references blur, futurist concepts and devices are mentioned without being explained, prose and poetry bond, details abound, and information density increases exponentially. The outcome is a linguistic maximalism that triggers multiple meanings. Gibson confronts the reader with so much *gomi* that he or she must sort through it selectively, choosing this
over that, supplying connections where no sure connections exist, often arriving at a conclusion about meaning that will differ to a fairly large degree from that arrived at by other readers.

Johnny, the protagonist, has stored espionage data for a gangster named Ralfi Face on a chip implanted in his brain. He goes to a bar intending to kill Ralfi, having heard Ralfi has put out a contract on him. Ralfi tells him the data came from someone who stole it from the Yakuza, the Japanese mob, which itself probably stole it for ransom from the Ono-Sendai corporation. Molly, an early version of the hired gun who will play a central role in the Trilogy, makes her first appearance when she suddenly intervenes, significantly showing up out of the darkness, hoping to make money by protecting Johnny. A Yakuza assassin murders Ralfi, but Molly and Johnny escape into Nighttown, a fringe society under the three southern-most kilometers of a geodesic dome in the Sprawl. There they first visit a dolphin named Jones, suggestive of those almost human ones in Mooney's *Easy Travel to Other Planets*, who with its jacked-up sonar reads the code for releasing the information stored on Johnny's chip. Then they visit a pirate broadcaster who records the stolen program and transmits a message to the Yakuza telling them to call off the assassin or Johnny and Molly will broadcast the data. The Yakuza assassin who killed Ralfi catches up with them far above Nighttown, among the dim labyrinthian world inhabited by the Lo Teks, a group of savage youths akin to those in Golding's *Lord of the Flies*. Molly murders the assassin on the ritual Killing Floor, she and Johnny become partners and lovers, and the story seems to conclude. But in *Neuromancer* the reader will learn that the Yakuza didn't forgive or forget. They simply bided their time before taking revenge. Having given Johnny and Molly several years to gain a false sense of security, they sent an assassin to kill the former, thus punishing the latter (chap. 15).

I "Johnny Mnemonic," the reader pierces the overwhelmingly vast, powerful, and mysterious web of multinational corporations like Ono-Sendai and gangster rings like the Yakuza. Like the Tristero in *The Crying of Lot 49*, these are "magic, anonymous and malignant."[4] Betrayal, violation, and ruthless manipulation are key themes, underscored here by images of disguise. Johnny has had plastic surgery and calls himself Edward Bax. Ralfi Face, whose very name implies false identity, has been altered to look like a once-famous rock'n'roll star. Molly's mirrorshades mask her eyes, her mechanically altered fingertips her scalpels, the Yakuza assassin's artificial thumb his weapon. The cyborg dolphin, a drug addict from the war, is encrusted in armor, and its skull has been deformed to house two large sensors. The Magnetic Dog Sisters, bouncers at the bar where Johnny meets Ralfi, have made themselves identical through cosmetic surgery, and another Dog, the fifteen-year-old Lo Tek who lives above Nighttown, wears fangs, scars, and a gaping eye socket that form "a mask of total bestiality." These images suggest the idea of chic vanity turned horrific, the belief in humans as animals, and the objective correlative between internal and external disfigurement. The last of these shares in the Southern tradition of the grotesque that evinces subjective malformation through objective malformation. Johnny's mind has been invaded and deformed by the chips within it just as his body has been invaded and deformed by plastic surgery. He has become a data-storage techno-centaur that literally lives off of other people's memories. Like most of the other characters in this fiction, he has become something less than human. It is appropriate, then, that most of the story takes place in and above Nighttown, a term taken from James Joyce's *Ulysses* (1922), a metaphor for the dark, irrational, and reptilian part of the human brain.

"Hinterlands" (1981) is another examination of invasion. This time, however, emphasis falls on cultural rather than individual trespass. Through extensive use of flashback, two plotlines converge. The first centers on the past life and death of Lieutenant Colonel Olga Tovyevski, a Soviet cosmonaut whose spaceship disappeared — apparently into another dimension — en route to Mars. When it suddenly reappeared two years later, the rescue team found Tovyevski insane. In her right fist, she clutched an extraterrestrial seashell. She was made into a martyr, while the CIA and KGB joined forces to find what lay beyond the magic entry point in space referred to as the Highway. Their attempts failed. Recording instruments came back blank. Astronauts who followed Tovyevski's path either committed suicide or went mad before they could be debriefed. The second plotline centers on the present attempt by the CIA and KGB to provide returning astronauts with an orbital womb-like environment called Heaven and a series of psychological surrogates. These surrogates are designed to ease the astronauts' reentry into this world, enabling them to report what they have seen. One surrogate, Toby Halpert, prepares to decondition an astronaut named Leni Hofmannstahl, only to find she too has killed herself.

At the heart of this fiction lies the realization of human ignorance. The CIA and KGB try to uncover the nature of the beyond, of a radically different and advanced culture, yet all they ultimately uncover is their own uncertainty about matters of knowing and being. As Toby comes to realize, their attempts at understanding the Highway are analogous to those of flies in an international airport that by chance blunder onto flights going to exotic countries, unaware of where they are travelling, how, or why. "Flies are advised not to ask too many questions," Toby reminds himself. "Flies are advised not to try for the Big Picture." Such tries lead, not to truth, but to the creation of fictions, "like those poor suckers on their island, who spend all their time building landing strips to make the big silver birds come back." Such attempts lead, as with the cargo-cults, to the creation of false metaphysics and religion. Consequently, Olga Tovyevski is martyred although she is no more than an insane cosmonaut. Heaven proves to be a fake, filled with recorded birdsongs, artificial trees, and plaster alps. Humankind, advanced as it might appear to be, is only a "hinterland tribe . . . looking for scraps," forced, like Parker in "Fragments of a Hologram Rose," to live with pieces in the absence of wholes. The only real knowledge, Toby comes to understand, is of the Fear, "the very hollow of night, an emptiness cold and implacable," a Conradian existential terror before chaos, meaninglessness, uncertainty, ignorance, and death.

Piggy-backing the plotline of the gangster heist (itself one more example of the invasion tale), "Burning Chrome" (1982) again moves out of the realm of spotless space stations, vague alternate universes, and reptilian aliens, and into the realm of a grungy near-future, crisp details, and high-tech lowlifes. Gibson thereby begins to develop his distinctive insignia, writing about the matrix simulator, prototype for cyberspace; Tom Maddox's creation, ICE, or Intrusion Countermeasures Electronics; the techno-centaur in the guise of Jack Automatic and his myoelectric arm, Rikki Wildside and her Zeiss Ikon eyes; the surgical boutique; the simstim deck; World War III as an event already in the past; and the puppet house, where prostitutes work drugged three-hour shifts in an approximation of REM sleep. He also creates the forerunners of four characters who will play significant roles in the Trilogy: Bobby Quine, the aging twenty-eight-year-old console cowboy, who shares much with Bobby Newmark; Rikki, who will become part Mona and part Angie; Finn, the seedy fence; and Tally Isham, the simstim star.

The theme again involves betrayal, violation, and manipulation. Bobby Quine and Jack Automatic exhibit only vestigial emotion and morality as they break into Chrome's computer system, rob the child-faced witch with cold gray eyes, destroy her power base, and as much as murder her by sapping her of her ability to defend herself against her enemies.[5] Bobby and Jack use Rikki Wildside, a naive teenager who sells her body to a puppet house to make enough money to buy a fashionable pair of new eyes and fly to Hollywood in the hopes of becoming a simstim star. Jack buys a Russian virus-program from Finn, who in turn bought it from someone who apparently killed the program's original thief. Using that program, Bobby violates Chrome's computer system. He uses the communication web to subvert the communication web. Jack helps Bobby violate Chrome while also betraying his friendship with Bobby by having an affair with Rikki. Rikki betrays her love affairs with Bobby and Jack by selling her body in the puppet house. In metaphorical rapes, Bobby and Jack penetrate Chrome's computer defenses, and Rikki's psychological ones, to drain them of their strength. Ironically, although much is made of Chrome's cold gray eyes and Rikki's beautiful new blue ones, both characters are blind to what happens to them. Each character, devoid of genuine human connections, is motivated by a ruthless need for control, be it in the form of money for Bobby and Chrome, or of simstim fame for Rikki. Each attempts to manipulate others to attain his or her goal. Bobby attempts to teach Rikki about the "wild side" of life, "the tricky wiring on the dark underside of things," but it is perhaps Jack who learns the most about this. In the end, he is the only character to feel a residual moral disgust when he realizes they have just murdered Chrome and allowed Rikki to go into prostitution. In a gesture of expiation, he uses some of the money he has just stolen to pay for a first-class ticket for Rikki to her dreamland. This is too little too late, but it is the best such characters can do.

Written with Bruce Sterling, "Red Star, Winter Orbit" (1983) represents a step back into fairly conventional science fiction. It is clearly much more the product of Sterling's imagination than Gibson's, as Gibson admits. "Bruce sent me a long version of the story," he recalls, "one that I essentially edited. It was more of an editing job. I shortened it. I rewrote it, but it mostly involved removing segments."[6] Elderly Colonel Korolev, first man on Mars, finds the Soviets have decided to scrap Kosmograd, the space station he has lived on for twenty years. Korolev and six of the thirty-two-member crew go on strike to protest the shutdown, but to no avail. In the final scene, Korolev, now the sole survivor on the space station, waits for Kosmograd to burn in Earth's atmosphere. He begins to hallucinate, and in what Gibson has called a kind of

"Heinlein dream," Korolev witnesses the invasion of the space station by a set of merry young American spacesquatters.[7]

Initially, the story appears to be about a new generation overtaking an old. Like Johnny Mnemonic, Korolev lives in other people's memories. While he often wants to remember the high point of his life, the Mars voyage, all he can do is recall media representations of it. Like the "popping, humming, and wheezing" space station on which he lives, Korolev is outdated. He is arthritic, suffers from calcium loss, listens to music from his childhood in the 1980's, and inhabits the Museum of the Soviet Triumph in Space. Opposed to him are the energetic young adulterous couple who continually make love and the Americans who, in the end, overrun the space station. But upon closer examination, the Soviets less represent youth than the aged gravity of pragmatism, believing that space is "a dream that failed." "We have no need to be here," one cosmonaut tells Korolev. Opposed to them, Korolev is then associated with the "wonderful lunacy" of the Americans who are idealistic and industrious visionaries. "You have to *want* a frontier — want it in your bones," one says. The story thereby comes to suggest the struggle between static prosaism (the winter orbit of death) and vital idealism (the burning red star). Which vision ultimately wins out depends on how the reader views the story's conclusion. If Korolev actually sees Americans enter the station, idealism is shown to triumph as it is passed from one generation to the next. If Korolev simply hallucinates his visitors, idealism is shown to be a sham, the hallucination of a dying way of life.[8] Once more a dualistic gesture, the authors keep both possibilities open at once.

If "Burning Chrome" is a blueprint for *Neuromancer*, then, "New Rose Hotel" (1984) is one for *Count Zero*. The third of the Sprawl series, its plot concerns corporate defection. An unnamed narrator waits to be murdered in a small sleeping compartment (appropriately called a "coffin") in a Japanese hotel. He passes time by recalling the events that led up to his current situation. He addresses his tale to Sandii, his lover and betrayer. It turns out that Maas Biolabs, a multinational corporation, hired the narrator and a man called Fox, a middleman in corporate crossovers, to bring Hiroshi Yomiuri, an important genetic engineer, from Maas Biolabs to Hosaka. The narrator and Fox in turn hired Sandii, a beautiful and seemingly naive young woman, to seduce Hiroshi in a Viennese hotel. The plan seemed successful at first. Hiroshi fell for Sandii and defected one October afternoon. But soon it became evident something had gone wrong. Someone had sabotaged Hiroshi's research project. The saboteur turned out to be Sandii. She had been secretly hired by Maas Biolabs to shortcircuit Hiroshi's defection. Instead of meeting the narrator at the New Rose Hotel when everything had blown over as she promised, Sandii introduced a deadly meningial virus program into Hiroshi's DNA synthesizer and then vanished. In a conventional plot twist, then, the Fox is outfoxed. The victimizers become victims. Having evaporated their credit, Hosaka sent assassins to kill Fox and the narrator. It succeeded in the first case. In the second, as with Johnny in "Johnny Mnemonic," it is only a matter of time. The story ends as Hosaka's deadly helicopter zeros in on the New Rose Hotel where the narrator is waiting.

We again meet the by-now familiar themes of betrayal, violation, and manipulation. But instead of Chrome's relatively small business or even the vast and powerful Ono-Sendai and Yakuza, here the reader finds what Fox calls "corporation as life form." If an alien were to come to Earth intending to identify the dominant form of intelligence on the planet, Fox claims, it would have to choose the multinational whose "structure is independent of the individual lives that comprise it." The multinational's blood is information, not individuals. Humans like Hiroshi become merchandise to be guarded, stolen, and destroyed. If the guiding metaphor in "Burning Chrome" is human-as-prostitute, and in "Johnny Mnemonic" human-as-animal, here it is human-as-commodity.

As if to underscore this point, Gibson emphasizes how little identity each of the characters has. Sandii reveals a new past each time she tells her history, "and always the one, you swore, that was really and finally the truth." She becomes, as Fox understands, no more than "ectoplasm, a ghost called up by the extremes of economies." Fox, a romantic figure searching for the Edge just as Gentry in *Mona Lisa Overdrive* will search for the Shape, is no better off. In an image reminiscent of Gibson's first story, Fox often empties his wallet late at night, "shuffling through his identification. He'd lay the pieces out in different patterns, rearrange them, wait for a picture to form." The narrator's past has also sunk into oblivion, "lost with all hands, no trace." Significantly, we never learn his name. After the defection he adopts a new identity as easily as he has done innumerable times before. The very story he narrates is an attempt to create a viable past through the act of telling, but for all the reader knows, it may be no more reliable than those tales manufactured by Sandii, Fox, or even Hosaka itself which quickly erases the other players from its corporate memory when its espionage plot fails. Each of the characters, then, is a kind of artist intent on producing a fiction, a cosmos out of chaos. But in each case Gibson reminds readers that art, like Sandii, always promises the tale that is really and finally the truth, only to fail forever to deliver the goods. In "New Rose Hotel," whose title (like that of "Fragments of a Hologram Rose") perverts traditional associations of the flower with love, innocence, and purity, chaos remains chaos. Art proves futile, memory defective, relationships impossible, humans ruthless, and selfhood unstable.

"Dogfight" (1985), written with Michael Swanwick, touches upon many of the previously discussed themes. It explores betrayal, violation, manipulation, the impossibility of human connection, and the role of the techno-centaur. It carries with it the feel of the Sprawl series in its emphasis on the dingy near-future, sharp details, and seedy high-tech lowlifes. But it is also the first story by Gibson to examine in depth the mind/body dualism suggested by ASP in "Fragments of a Hologram Rose," cyberspace in "Burning Chrome," and data-storage chips in "Johnny Mnemonic." Deke, a down-and-out petty thief and drifter, has been exiled from Washington, D.C., for shoplifting. He takes a bus as far as Tidewater, Virginia, where he finds a gameroom filled with people playing Spads & Fokkers, a new kind of 3-D video involving antique planes. Fascinated, Deke steals a projective wetware wafer housing the game from a nearby giftshop. He rents a room in a tenement and meets Nance Bettendorf, a well-off student wetware wiz who offers to upgrade his game so he can play against the pros. The extra edge Deke needs to win comes, not from his own determination and skill, but from a military drug called hype that increases reflexes and concentration. Nance scores two hits of it and Deke bullies her out of one, thereby wrecking her college career since she needs both hits for a project on which she is working. Then he heads to a bar where he challenges the Spads & Fokkers champ, Tiny Montgomery, a crippled combat vet who, with the help of hype flew in a South American war. Spads & Fokkers is Tiny's life. Deke raises large bets, beats him, and ends virtually where he began: alone, inhumane, a thief, and a drifter. His only dim revelation is that he no longer has anyone with whom to recount his tale of fraud and victory.

As with ASP and cyberspace, characters who jack into Spads & Fokkers leave their bodies behind and lose themselves in a mental landscape. The drug-like result is "so perfect, so *true*" it makes the material world around one "look like an illusion." Accordingly, people abandon the decadence of the body and penetrate the brilliance of the mind. When Deke steps off the bus in Tidewater, he notices his legs feel "like wood" and seem "to have died already." He lives in poverty and hunger. Tiny too has bad legs. He is confined to a wheelchair, having been shot down over Bolivia and crippled with high doses of hype that have led to brain cell attenuation. The police have put a brainlock on Deke so he cannot bear the idea of returning to Washington, and Nance's parents have put a chastity lock on her so that she cannot bear the idea of being touched by another human. The characters, then, cannot control their own bodies. Just as the beautiful erotic images Nance produces with her projective wetware are trapped within flame, so each character's brilliant mental essence is trapped within flesh. Deke, Tiny, and Nance are artists who use their creations to transcend the ugliness of the material world. This is what makes Deke's final victory over Tiny so cruel. Their dogfight is not one between toys, but between imaginations. Deke both robs Tiny of his title and of his method for escaping his deformed body. After winning, Deke wants to tell everyone the story of his success, "going over the victory time and again, contradicting himself, making up details, laughing and bragging." Yet, like the narrator of "New Rose Hotel," he no longer has anyone with whom to share his tale. He has used the very people who might have listened to win his egotistic and destructive game. He may think he has just triumphed for the first time in his life, but his victory has been dishonest and ruthlessly self-serving.

"The Winter Market" (1986) also contemplates the role of the artist. Whereas "Dogfight" emphasizes the artist's ability to transcend the material world, "The Winter Market" emphasizes the pain the artist must endure in that world before transcendence. Casey, the narrator, is an editor of simstim recordings at a company called Autonomic Pilot.[9] Through Rubin Stark, a sculptor-friend, he meets Lise, a sensitive and angry down-and-out woman with Hollywood aspirations who, because of a congenital disease, is confined to a polycarbon exoskeleton. Impressed by the intensity of Lise's feelings, Casey introduces her to the recording industry and helps edit her first simstim, *Kings of Sleep*, which turns out to be a success. Her health deteriorates, partially as the result of her disease, partially of her addiction to a drug called wizz. Before she dies, she enters her personality construct into a computer so that she can continue to make art from beyond the grave, a plot that forms the basis of *Neuromancer*.

Gibson presents two views of art in "The Winter Market." One is romantic, one postmodern. Lise represents the former. When Casey listens to her voice, he hears "levels of pain there, and subtlety, and an amazing cruelty." She is literally isolated from others, living in her exoskeleton, helpless without it. She is self-absorbed, able only to take from rather than give to others, unable to make love. She is self-destructive as well, refusing to tend to the sores on her wrists caused by the exoskeleton, or to her addiction to wizz. When Casey jacks into her mind, he is so startled and moved by what he feels that he cannot stop himself from crying. Like the characters in "Dogfight," her deformed body is controlled by forces outside herself, but her imagination is dark brilliance. Unlike Rubin, she is "able to break the surface tension, dive down deep, down and out, out into Jung's sea, and bring back ... dreams." Like Rikki, Tiny, and Sandii, she uses her talent to buy her way out of this world. She escapes her body and enters the purity of cyberspace, but, like Coretti in "The Belonging Kind," she ironically finds peace only by sacrificing her humanity.

The postmodern view of art is represented by Rubin Stark. A *gomi no sensei*, he never likes to refer to himself as an artist. A predecessor of Slick Henry in *Mona Lisa Overdrive*, he wanders the city "like some vaguely benign Satan" gathering junk to make whimsical deconstructive robotic sculptures suggestive of those produced by Mark Pauline's Survival Research Laboratories. Childlike, he is not overly concerned about success, and he does not take his art especially seriously. For Rubin, as for Gibson at this point in his career, art is fun, no more than a "defective toy." Art enables him to maintain his sanity and his humanity.

To sum up briefly, then, the stories in *Burning Chrome* mark Gibson's movement from experimentation at the level of technique to experimentation at the level of idea. They evince his gradual evolution of near-future geography that will become his signature in the Matrix Trilogy. Throughout the course of these fictions, the reader can chart the rise of thematic complexity, the paradigmatic American character, emotional depth and resonance, and linguistic density. A number of characters who will surface in Gibson's major work make their initial appearance here. Many themes which will become central to Gibson's project also occur for the first time. These themes include the impossibility of real human connection, the instability of selfhood, the megacorporation as life form, the human as commodity and techno-centaur, the role of the artist, the role of memory, mind/body dualism, the suspicion of normalcy, betrayal, violation, and manipulation.

Endnotes

1. Jospeh Nicholas and Judith Hanna, "William Gibson," *Interzone* 1.13 (1985), 18.
2. Carol McGuirk, "The 'New' Romancers: Science Fiction Innovators from Gernsback to Gibson," paper delivered at the Fiction 2000 conference at the University of Leeds, June 28-July 1, 1989. Gibson asserts his use of Campbell's "Twilight" was unconsious on his part.
3. Takayuki Tatsumi, "An Interview with William Gibson," in *Science Fiction Eye* 1.1 (Winter 1987), 16.
4. Thomas Pynchon, *The Crying of Lot 49* (New York: Bantam, 1966), 11.
5. Gibson feels my reading of these characters is too harsh.
6. Tatsumi, 16.
7. Ibid., 16.
8. Sterling and Gibson did not intend the second reading, in which Korolev hallucinates his visitors.
9. "Autonomic Pilot" is a phrase donated by Lewis Shiner.

Neuromancer

Watch out for worlds behind you.
—Lou Reed, "Sunday Morning"

When Gibson wrote the short story "Burning Chrome," he still felt he was at least four or five years away from beginning a novel. But Terry Carr, editor of the newly resurrected Ace Science Fiction Specials series, had other ideas. He approached Gibson and asked him to do a book. Carr felt much current science fiction was "simply skilled," "timid and literarily defensive" (*N*, preface). He was on the lookout for young SF writers with promise, aesthetic quality, and vivid extrapolative imaginations who would revitalize the series which in its first incarnation had brought forth work by such authors as Ursula K. LeGuin, Joanna Russ, and Roger Zelazny. Without much forethought, Gibson said yes and almost immediately regretted his decision. "I was *terrified* once I actually sat down and started to think about what this meant," he says. "It had been taking me something like three months to write a short story, so starting something like this was really a major leap."[1]

To assuage his fears, Gibson sought a familiar narrative structure with which he would feel comfortable working. After some thought, he settled upon the gangster-heist plot, although he admits he "never had a very clear idea of what was going to happen in the end, except [that his characters] had to *score big*."[2] He also looked back to his short stories to discover what he felt had worked so far and decided he would combine Molly's character from "Johnny Mnemonic" with the environment and general narrative outline from "Burning Chrome." "Very much under the influence of Robert Stone," he generated tough characters who maneuver at the fringes of a violent society filled with addictions and paranoid conspiracies.[3] Afraid of losing the reader's attention, he decided to make the book into "a roller-coaster ride" with "a hook on every page."[4] As he began his project, he stumbled upon another problem; he sensed a good deal of what he was writing was comprised of "shabbier coincidences."[5] To take care of this impression, he ended up reworking the first two-thirds of his manuscript a dozen times. Once he began to have a feel for the universe he was producing and to be more confident of his technique, he also went back and made many stylistic changes. Over time, his manuscript became increasingly shorter, denser, and more complicated.

The result was his most important, artistically successful, and critically acclaimed novel: *Neuromancer* (1984). Like the *Odyssey*, it is epic or global in perspective, taking place in Japan, Amsterdam, Paris, Istanbul, high orbit, and the Sprawl in a country Gibson is careful never to identify as the United States. Like the *Odyssey*, it involves a number of quests, although here the magical and monstrous universe of the Mediterranean is replaced by that of cyberspace and the heroic Ulysses by the antiheroic Henry Dorsett Case. And, like the *Odyssey*, it is divided into twenty-four sections, suggestive of the completeness of the Greek alphabet that encompasses all from alpha to omega. But here the similarities between the premodern epic and the postmodern novel end. The former is the product of an integrated culture that has a strong sense of morality, hierarchy, and totality, while the latter is the product of a disintegrated culture that knows only amorality, contradiction, and heterogeneous change.

An emblem of this disintegrated culture, *Neuromancer*'s plot is filled with dazzling (and often confusing) twists and turns. It might, therefore, be helpful to spend a moment unravelling the book's narrative. Gibson groups the twenty-four smaller sections into four larger ones plus a brief coda; this form mimics the five-act structure of the brutal Senecan revenge tragedy.

The first large section, "Chiba City Blues" (chapters 1-2), is set in the world of Night City. The environment is reminiscent of Pynchon's Zone of irrationality in *Gravity's Rainbow*, an underworld where all fences are down and one way as good as another. Here Molly collects Case, a once top-notch computer cowboy now bent on self-destruction, and brings him to Armitage with whom he makes a deal: Armitage fixes Case's nervous system, which has been destroyed by Case's former employers as punishment for his trying to doublecross them, on the condition that Case will do a job for Armitage.[6] At the end of this part, Linda Lee, Case's ex-girlfriend who stole hot information from him in order to gain his attention, is suddenly and mysteriously murdered, though by whom and why remain unclear.

The second and third sections involve preparations for the job Case agrees to do for Armitage. "The Shopping Expedition" (chapters 3-7) is set first in the Sprawl, then Istanbul. Case and Molly break into the Sense/Net data-storage library to steal Dixie Flatline's computer construct, famous for its ability to crack ICE. Next Case, Armitage, and Molly travel to Istanbul to enlist the talents of Peter Riviera, a ruthless Aryan, infamous for his ability to project holograms of other people's fears and desires. Meanwhile, Case and Molly discover that an artificial intelligence in Berne called Wintermute is behind Armitage's plans. The third section, "Midnight in the Rue Jules Verne" (chapters 8-12), takes place in high orbit on Freeside, a Las Vegas-like pleasure dome, and the nearby Zion cluster, where Armitage, Molly, Case, and Riviera make their final arrangements for what they now learn will be an assault on Straylight, enclave of the Tessier-Ashpools, an eccentric, wealthy and inbred high orbit clan.

In the fourth part, "The Straylight Run" (chapters 13-23), the quartet moves toward the labyrinthan core of Straylight, back into an underworld zone of irrationality, suggestive of Night City in the book's opening chapters. Case is arrested, but Wintermute kills the police guarding him. Armitage suffers a mental breakdown, and Wintermute murders him as well. Molly accidentally stumbles upon Ashpool, the clan's patriarch, in the midst of a suicide attempt; when he threatens her, she kills him. But she is soon kidnapped by Riviera who has found 3Jane, the last Tessier-Ashpool left awake and alive in Straylight (most of the others have been cryogenically frozen; Jean, 3Jane's brother, is on earth doing business). Riviera, having served his purpose of befriending 3Jane with his magical projections and gaining access to Straylight, has decided to doublecross Armitage and Wintermute. Case, who has been monitoring the situation through his cyberspace deck and simstim unit on the Zion cluster, heads in with a rastafarian named Maelcum to rescue Molly. Hideo, 3Jane's ninja servant, murders Riviera shortly after Case and Maelcum appear. 3Jane gives Case the password that will allow Wintermute to attain its goal: to merge with Neuromancer, another Tessier-Ashpool AI, which has fought against the union. The two AIs can now dominate the matrix.

In the brief coda, "Departure and Arrival" (chapter 24), Molly leaves Case. Case returns to the Sprawl where he buys a new cyberspace deck, settles down to his old life as computer cowboy, and finds a girlfriend named Michael. Ulysses comes home. Although he loses a Circe-Calypso, he gains a Penelope. Following the myth of the hero, and of renaissance comedy, Gibson apparently provides the reader with a happy ending; integration follows on the heels of separation and education.

The essence of the plot, then, becomes clear. Both John Harness Ashpool and his wife, Marie-France Tessier, have made bids for immortality. Ashpool has placed his faith in cryogenics. His bid fails, however, in part because of sabotage on his daughter 3Jane's part. Tessier, on the other hand, has built the two AIs, Wintermute and Neuromancer, and has placed her personality construct in the latter. Although Ashpool murders her, a version of her survives. Over the years, Wintermute begins illegally doing deals on its own, programmed to join with its other half in order to attain tremendous power. The result is that Case, Molly, Riviera, Armitage, 3Jane, and most of the other humans in the novel become Wintermute's pawns. It brutally manipulates them, often murdering those in its way, always feeding others' fears and addictions to attain its goal of union with Neuromancer.

Outlining such a complex plot, one is wise to keep in mind Jean-Paul Sartre's caveat apropos of his attempt to summarize Faulkner's *The Sound and the Fury* (1929): to simplify a narrative is to invent a narrative the author did not intend. While linear readings like the above are necessary for gaining a greater understanding of what happens in a book as complicated and sometimes mystifying as *Neuromancer*, Gibson's novel almost immediately begins shortcircuiting such confident mappings by generating textual ambiguity and instability at a number of strata. A register of this is the novel's title. The word *Neuromancer* is Gibson's own invention and, while it carries virtually no denotative charge (save for the fictional AI to which it refers in the text), it is rich in connotations. In fact, many of the novel's key concerns and themes reside within it.

First, the title hints at the novel's *new romanticism*, which embraces innovation and emotion. Often this impulse takes the form of an intense subjective expressionism. It is particularly evinced in the cyberspace sequences that recall the final wild psychedelic moments of Kubrick's *2001: A Space Odyssey* (1968), and, though with a much more disorienting feel, the dynamic and colorful land of Fleming's Oz (1938) set against a static and blank Kansas. Ironically, while the characters in the text are emotionally bankrupt, they exist in environments that are emotionally charged for the reader. Readers need only think of Molly's high-paced invasion of Sense/Net or Case's fragmented recollection of the operation to restore his nervous system.

Further, the novel partakes in a new romantic longing for the absolute. Cyberspace, like the black monolith in Kubrick's *2001* and Oz in Fleming's film, represents a frontier of consciousness. Case is a 24-year-old Ulysses of cyberspace whom Ratz, the bartender at the Chat, continually refers to mockingly as "the artiste." A metaphor for the Byronic outlaw-writer who lives in his memory and imagination, Case continually strives for the transcendent reality locked within his computer console. Often going days without eating or washing, seldom sleeping, he leaves the mundane material world of "meat" behind and voyages through a purer landscape of the mind. There he encounters one visionary experience after another, including death itself. Like Faust, however, he has sold his soul to the devil to do so. His Mephistopheles is Armitage, his Satan Wintermute. More in keeping with Tennyson's than Homer's Ulysses, Case never reaches the end of his quest. Although he returns home at the conclusion of his mission, he is beckoned on into the vast steps of data by Neuromancer, Linda Lee's and Dixie Flatline's construct, and even some version of himself which wanders through the matrix. Like the protagonist in Tennyson's "Ulysses," he understands it is not too late to seek a newer world. Wintermute and Neuromancer also strive for a transcendent reality: cosmic unity. But they fail to attain their goal as well. At the moment of transcendence, as the reader will learn in *Count Zero*, they fracture into manifold gods or subprograms, unable and unwilling to continue as a perfect form. Along the same lines, Ashpool and Tessier long for immortality; the former certainly fails, killed by Molly in the midst of a suicide attempt, and the latter, depending on how one defines selfhood, possibly fails. The *new* romanticism, then, is not ultimately about attaining the absolute. Rather, it is about the failure to do so. It is less about end than process. Like the Duchamp assemblage Molly comes across in the Straylight enclave, the suitors can never (and perhaps *should* never) reach the bride.

Second, as Porush notes, the title echoes "*necromancer*, the magician who conjures up the dead."[7] No doubt this is a text inhabited by those raised from the dead, reborn, from Dixie Flatline in the form of a construct to Linda Lee's structure in cyberspace. Ashpool intermittently awakes from his cryogenic death-sleep, and the child 3Jane perceives Wintermute as a ghost whispering in her ear. Case flatlines and comes back to talk about it. Metaphorically, Corto is reborn when he is transformed into Armitage.

But Porush does not point out a secondary "necromancy" in the title. Not only are characters raised from the dead by a number of fictional magicians, but also various genres are "raised from the dead" by the very real magician of magicians — Gibson himself. The text is one about regeneration and endurance. Forms arise, undergo transformations, and continue metamorphosed. Gibson becomes the *new romancer* behind *Neuromancer*, revitalizing the science-fiction novel, the quest story, the myth of the hero, the mystery, the hard-boiled detective novel, the epic, the thriller, and the tales of the cowboy and romantic artist, among others. He represents old stories in a revealing revamped, intertexual pastiche.

Third, as Porush notes, the title "puns on the idea of the literary text as a cybernetic manipulation of the human cortex, a 'neurological romance.'"[8] The novel, that is, is a kind of textual machine that activates and stimulates the human mind. It thus functions much like cyberspace does with respect to characters within the novel. In this sense, *Neuromancer* is no more than any other fiction: a "neurological romance."

Porush does not point out that the metaphor of neurological romance suggests one of the major themes of the novel: the interface between human and machine. Just as the reader's mind is ingested by the text, so too are the humans in the text ingested by the AI's. In the ritual act of cannibalism, Wintermute and Neuromancer make them into so much "meat." This raises questions of freewill, re-visions of the human, and Gibson's attitude toward technology. It asks us for a consideration of selfhood: *where is a person's mind? what is it? what is the relationship between brain (circuitry) and mind (thought and feeling)? and how long and under what conditions does it remain a person's mind before subtly becoming something other than that?* Is, for instance, Dixie Flatline's construct, which behaves exactly as Dixie Flatline ought to behave, still Dixie Flatline, or something other (less or more?) than Dixie Flatline? Intuition may give one answer, reason another. To this extent, Gibson becomes a *neuro-mancer*. He becomes a prophet (*mancy* derives from the Greek word *manteia*, or *divination*, which in turn derives from the Greek word *mantis*, or *prophet*) of the mind/brain (*neuro* derives from the Greek word *neuron*, or *nerve*).

The human, Gibson's prophecy runs, has transmuted into a techno-centaur. By jacking into his cyberspace deck, Case merges with and hence becomes, in part, a machine. Molly not only sports implanted mirrorshades and scalpel-blades under her fingernails, but also a jacked-up nervous system and a fair amount of silicon in her head. When she walks down the sardonically named Memory Lane, she notices all the teenagers wear up to a dozen carbon sockets sprouting from behind their ears. Riviera has an implant in his lung cavity that aids in his holographic projections, and Armitage is a personality constructed by a computer from an autistic ruin. McCoy Pauley took his nickname, Dixie Flatline, from his interface with a computer. Now he (it?) is a construct, a cybernaut. Like Slothrop in *Gravity's Rainbow*, he possesses virtually no temporal bandwidth; he experiences time as a series of *nows*. Yet he talks and thinks just as McCoy Pauley would talk and think. When Case asks him if he possesses sentience as well, Dixie Flatline answers that it *feels* like he does. "But I'm really just a bunch of ROM," he adds. "It's one of them, ah, philosophical questions, I guess . . . . But I ain't likely to write you no poem, if you follow me. Your AI, it just might. But it ain't in no way *human*" (chap. 10).

Or is it? Humans in Gibson's novel tend to act like machines while the machines tend to act like humans. Characters, such as Molly and Armitage, for instance, exhibit limited internal action in the form of thoughts and feelings. They come closer, in fact, to acting like highly complicated automata. They seldom ponder ideas. They cannot love. And they cannot even hate in a traditional sense. Case experiences short bursts of rage, of course, but these are closer to animalistic explosions than to human emotions. As a rule, he feels virtually nothing. "He'd been numb a long time, years," it occurs to him. "All his nights down Ninsei, his nights with Linda, numb in bed and numb at the cold sweating center of every drug deal." When he does finally feel a flash of anger, his first reaction is to think: "*It's the meat talking, ignore it*" (chap. 12). Wintermute, on the other hand, is driven by a passionate longing to connect with its other half. It schemes, betrays, and murders, not out of reflex or circuitry, but out of deep desire.

By posing such questions *Are humans simply highly complicated robots?* and *Can machines feel and desire?*, Neuromancer joins a philosophical conversation that has been going on since the seventeenth century. In 1641, Descartes asserted that the human body should be considered a machine and that animals should be considered automata lacking thought and feeling. About one-hundred years later, Julien Offray de La Mettrie, a French physician and philosopher, combined these two ideas and extended Descartes' notions to include the human mind. We are, he said, no more than conscious machines. He thereby interrogated that part of us we conventionally hold most free. The other side of the equation — that machines can in fact think and exhibit purposive behavior — surfaced during the 1940s with the development of cybernetics. A British logician, A. M. Turing (hence the Turing Police in Gibson's novel), asserted in 1950 that it was theoretically possible to manufacture a thinking machine. Indeed, he said, in the future it would be possible to build a machine with intelligence and purposive behavior. Only human predjudice would prevent humanity from conceptualizing the resulting cybernetic construct as another human mind.

To the extent that Turing suggests that intelligence merely consists of a series of potentially well-distinguished tasks, he agrees with the characters in *Neuromancer* who are characterized by what they *do* rather than by what they *think* or *feel*. Lewis Shiner recalls Gibson talking about a college course he took on American Naturalism in which he read and was deeply impressed by Nelson Algren's *The Man With the Golden Arm* (1949), a text where characters are defined by external rather than internal action.[9] This impulse is reflected throughout *Neuromancer*, a text that privileges high-speed and often high-tech movement over static and low-tech contemplation. Molly registers this thrust when she claims: "Anybody any good at what they do, that's what they *are*, right?" (chap. 3). To be, according to Gibson, is to do. Action precedes essence.

Given this logic, a reader might arrive at the conclusion that Gibson's view of technology is negative at best. Technology is apparently that which dehumanizes, robs human capacity for thought and feeling. This turns out to be only part of the story, however. Gibson in fact claims to have a "neutral" stance toward technology. Perhaps "ambivalent" is closer to the mark. While he argues that "trying to ignore it would be like trying to ignore oxygen," Gibson feels his stance toward technology is not an either/or proposition. On the one hand, he is not anti-technological. On the other, he does not think "technology's going to straighten things out for us and get everything going".[10] He is both fascinated and fearful of technology's potential. In *Neuromancer*, one form of technology — cyberspace — stands as a gateway to a universe of visionary intensity. At the same time, it is also a tool used to control information and people. While it is true that Dixie Flatline attains a kind of immortality through technology, it is also true that the kind of immortality he attains is nightmarish; his only wish is that his program be erased when the job for Wintermute is finished. Moreover, technology tends to produce results different from, and more radical than, those intended by its creators. Wintermute, an AI designed to serve humans, has transfigured into a monster that manipulates them.

One therefore has to ask whether technology has freed Gibson's characters from the gravity of their environments in any way, or whether it has actually created a captivity for them heretofore undreamed of by humans. Most of Gibson's characters act the way they do, after all, not because they *want* to, but because they *have* to. They lack genuine free will. Molly asserts that she behaves as she does because she is "wired" that way. Case performs his job for Wintermute because he has been blackmailed; his nervous system has been repaired and then planted with toxin sacs that will dissolve and destroy it if he does not do what he is told. 3Jane and Hideo are the products of genetic engineering. Wintermute builds Armitage from Corto's remains and then uses him while controlling Riviera through drugs.

Like La Mettrie's conscious automata, then, the immachinated individual in Gibson's world does not govern him or herself. Rather, in a universe reminiscent of Kafka's and Pynchon's, humans are steered by larger bewildering and malignant forces. For Gibson, those forces tend to take the form of AI's or megacorporate entities whose weapons are information. Molly understands this as she and Case stroll through the gardens of Topkapi in Istanbul. She kicks a loose pebble into a pond filled with carp and aquatic flowers and watches the ripples spread from the center of impact. "We're out where the little waves are too broad," she says, "we can't see the rock that hit the center. We know something's there, but not why" (chap. 7). Just as the knife-fighters at Sammi's arena in Night City do battle as part of some corporate recreational project, so too do humans in Gibson's world play deadly games whose rules and rulers they do not comprehend.

Gibson captures these forces in the central image of the wasp nest. In a dream, Case recalls how as a teenager he burned a nest outside his apartment window when a wasp from it stung the girl with whom he was living. When he inspected the charred remains that had fallen into the alley below, he discovered a horror "hideous in its perfection": "the spiral birth factory, stepped terraces of the hatching cells, blind jaws of the unborn moving ceaselessly, the staged progress from egg to larva, near-wasp, wasp" (chap. 10). Later, Wintermute tells Case he projected that dream for him with a hologram rig to show what the Tessier-Ashpools aspired to. They strived to be corporation-as-lifeform, efficient and emotionless as machines, relentless and deadly as wasps going about the business of reproduction.

Like the wasp nest, the Tessier-Ashpool's home is a "parasitic structure" (chap. 19). Straylight sucks life out of Freeside in the same way the high orbit clan sucks life out of its corporate deals, humans who attempt to cross it, and even each other. Straylight is often associated with a gothic pirate's den, a fairy-tale witch's castle, and biblical Babylon itself. It is also a labyrinth, a mythic form that stands for initiation and education as well as solitude and ambiguity. From this perspective, Ashpool, 3Jane, and (later) Riviera become its minotaur, while Molly and Case become its Theseus. It carries distant associations with the accursed house of Atreus as well, enclosing a doomed clan filled with ruthless betrayal, deceit, madness, and murder. Ashpool, insane king, is over two-hundred years old; he has killed his wife and slit one of his daughter's throats after sleeping with her. 3Jane has sabotaged the program that controlled Ashpool's cryogenic system, thereby in effect killing him. The goals of the clan have failed. Over time it has experienced "a turning in." "We have sealed ourselves away behind our money, growing inward, generating a seamless universe of self," 3Jane comments (chap. 14). Autism pervades the Straylight world. The Tessier-Ashpools have, like another house of Atreus in Gabriel García Márquez's *One Hundred Years of Solitude* (1967), committed incest, the ultimate image of solitude, exclusion from community, impossibility of diversity and change, and radical egocentricism.

This brings us back again to questions of selfhood: *what is my relationship with the world? what am I? where do I stop and others begin? what constitutes human identity?* As we have seen, for Gibson the human self is unstable. It always teeters on the verge of becoming something inhumane and often inhuman. It can easily be destroyed by drugs, as Case realizes when he watches Linda Lee's "personality fragment, calving like an iceberg, splinters drifting away" (chap. 1). It can easily be altered by cosmetic surgery as with Angelo, the Panther Modern, whose "smooth and hideous" face is a graft grown on collagen and shark-cartilage polysaccharides. Selfhood frequently appears to be nothing more than forgery, whether it takes the form of Case's string of false passports, Armitage's handsome inexpressive mask covering Corto's insanity, or the Panther Moderns' camouflage suits. Humans are seldom what they seem in Gibson's world. Beneath the roles they play exists absence or horror. As Wintermute says, in one of his various pseudo-human incarnations: "I, insofar as I *have* an 'I' — this gets rather metaphysical, you see — I am the one who arranges things" (chap. 9). When discussing identity, language slips, syntax comes up short. Even Wintermute's sureness of purpose decomposes in a sentence that fractures as it attempts to articulate personality.

Interrogation of selfhood leads to interrogation of a related concern: the relationship between mind and body. Just as Dorothy momentarily abandons the uninteresting black-and-white universe of Kansas for the dazzling polychromatic one of Oz, so too do many of Gibson's characters abandon the polluted dark universe of the Sprawlworld for the pure multicolored one of cyberspace. By doing so, they move from the realm of *chronos* to the realm of *kairos*. That is, they move from a prosaic geography registering realistic chronology, logic, and stability, to a transcendent one registering fantastic timelessness, alogic, and possibility. Like their kindred spirit, Lewis Carroll's curious Alice, they head down the rabbit hole, eschewing the decadence of the body, and penetrate Wonderland, embracing the imaginative splendor of the mind.

Mind/body dualism initially seems to arrange itself along gender lines in *Neuromancer.* Reminiscent of D. H. Lawrence's schema, males tend to be associated with the former, females with the latter. Case is addicted to the mental landscape of the matrix and views his body as "meat." Dixie Flatline's construct is pure mind. Linda Lee, on the other hand, is perceived by Case as a body whose mind has been destroyed by drugs; she is a betrayer as well, having stolen his RAM, further underscoring the negative associations connected with the "meat" world. Molly represents pure body. Once a prostitute in a puppet house, she is now a hired gun. Because of her jacked-up nervous system, she possesses magnificent control over her reflexes. Through her scalpel blades and mirrorshades, she has transformed "meat" into art. Gibson sees her as a composite of Clint Eastwood, Bruce Lee, Emma Peel, and Chrissie Hynde.[11] McGuirk also recognizes in her the razorgirl from Fritz Leiber's "Coming Attraction,"[12] while Samuel Delany identifies her as a version of Jael from Joanna Russ's *The Female Man.*[13] Razorgirl sports both concealed eyes and steel fingernails; Jael wears black and possesses retractable claws. For Case, Molly is simply "every bad-ass hero" (chap. 18). Appropriately, then, she has had her tear ducts routed into her mouth so that she spits instead of cries. She becomes another incarnation of the hard, isolated, stoic, murderous American cowboy.

Here, however, the gender-specific arrangement of the mind/body dualism begins to break down. With Molly, Gibson has ironically imposed stereotypically male traits upon a female character. At the same time, he has also devalued those traits by implying they are part of the decadent material world that must be transcended by attaining cyberspace, an area of being to which only males have access in this novel. Gibson further complicates the question of gender by calling the sum total of cyberspace "the matrix." The word *matrix* derives from the Latin for *womb*, which in turn derives from the Latin for *mother.* So while it is true that only males have access to cyberspace, it is equally true that what they have access to is a female region. Add to this that console jockeys employ the sexual metaphor of "jacking in" when they speak of entering the matrix, and readers soon realize Gibson is not so much underscoring discrete genders as he is the search for a union of opposites. The male principle (Case, the computer cowboy, the mind) strives to join with the female principle (Molly, the cyberspace matrix, the body) to attain a sense of completeness. Case not only penetrates Molly sexually, but also merges with her by means of the simstim unit attached to his cyberspace deck. The couple performs most efficiently and successfully at the moment of fusion. Separated, they become vulnerable.

The quest for a union of opposites, for wholeness, is the key theme of *Neuromancer.* Case and Molly seek physical and metaphysical connection. Dixie Flatline conceives of himself as a combination of two brains, one in the head and one in the tailbone. Case tries to bond with Linda Lee early in the novel, while later he actually merges briefly with Neuromancer.

But the dominant manifestation of this theme takes the form of Wintermute's compulsive attempt to join with Neuromancer. Many years ago, the reader learns, Marie-France Tessier rejected the illusory immortality of cryogenics that Ashpool pursued. While freezing the body for long intervals and thawing it for short ones created the *appearance* of eternal life, Tessier soon realized the result was in fact simply to stretch time "into a series of warm blinks strung along a chain of winter" (chap. 24). She therefore decided to place her personality construct into an AI, Neuromancer. This would enable her to "live" forever in the same way Dixie Flatline "lives" forever. She also commissioned the construction of a second AI, Wintermute, which would take over the role of corporate decision-maker. This would enable the Tessier-Ashpool clan itself to become immortal. After Ashpool murdered Tessier, Wintermute began running the corporation on its own. Tessier, it turned out, had built into Wintermute the compulsion to free itself from reliance on others and to seek its other half. Wintermute, whose mainframe was in Berne, began plotting to link with Neuromancer, whose mainframe was in Rio. The nexus would be the Villa Straylight, clan headquarters. Wintermute is "hive mind," while Neuromancer is "personality" and hence "immortality" (chap. 24). In other words: Wintermute is reason, action, stereotypically male; Neuromancer is emotion, passive, stereotypically female. If in terms of Chinese philosophy Wintermute represents the force of *yang* in the universe, then Neuromancer represents the force of *yin*. Each suggests half the structure of the binary human mind, half the structure of cosmic totality. United, they become an all-powerful absolute, "the sum total of the works, the whole show" (chap. 24). They become the metanarrative of the matrix itself. Like a god, they become omniscient and omnipotent.

From one point of view, the Wintermute-Neuromancer plot concerns a universal quest for harmony, wholeness, and perfection. From quite another, it concerns the potential danger of out-of-control cybernetic entities. This second perspective is reinforced by a number of similar plotlines that cluster behind the one involving Wintermute-Neuromancer. Perhaps most important is Steven Lisberger's *Tron*. In this film, the techno-rebel protagonist, Flynn, battles a master computer obsessed with ingesting and thereby uniting with other programs to gain immense power and control in the matrix. Like Case, Flynn (whose name also invites comparison with Gibson's Finn) jacks into and briefly inhabits the matrix.[14] Another plotline echoed by the one involving Wintermute-Neuromancer is HAL's in Kubrick's *2001*, in which the master computer on the Jupiter mission begins doing deals on its own, murdering three cryogenically frozen crew members, killing a fourth outside the spacecraft, and trying to control the sole survivor for its own mysterious ends. HAL's plotline is emblematic of the many others that touch upon humans' fear of cybernetic or quasi-cybernetic entities running amok. All of them track back through the industrial revolution to the prototype located in Mary Shelley's *Frankenstein* (1818). Viewed in light of Shelley's work, Tessier is a Frankenstein who creates a monster to achieve eternal life. Like Frankenstein's creature, Wintermute longs for another of its species and will murder to find it. And, like Frankenstein himself, Tessier is a romantic Faustian figure who quests for the absolute and who is willing to make a pact with a demon to attain it. At the same time Gibson reinforces this plotline, he also reverses it: while a monstrous human (Tessier) creates a humanoid monster (Wintermute-Neuromancer), so too does a humanoid monster (Wintermute) create a monstrous human (Armitage). In each case, the romantic hope of perfection falls short. As in Shelley's novel, the creator loses control of its creation. Tessier dies, and Wintermute-Neuromancer tries to dominate the matrix, only to dis-

Count Zero) that it cannot maintain its perfect state. Wintermute's creature, Armitage, goes insane.

By fusing the monstrous and the human, the sane and the insane, Gibson not only questions the role of technology in contemporary society, the relationship between the body and mind, free will, gender, and selfhood. He also ups his stakes by ultimately questioning humanity itself: *to what extent is humanity truly a discrete and noble species, and to what extent is it simply a composite of other inhumane and inhuman beings?* Gibson often portrays the human form as part-beast. This runs the gamut from the metaphoric (Linda Lee's eyes are like those "of some animal pinned in the headlights of an oncoming vehicle" [chap. 1]) to the literal (the brutal Panther Moderns wear canine toothbud implants). He also frequently employs the *grotechsque*, a combination of the grotesque and high-tech, to indicate that humans are comic-horrific automata. An example of this may be found in Ratz. His name hints at his ties with the animal kingdom, but his prosthetic arm and steel teeth firmly link him with the universe of cybernetics. At a time when cosmetic surgery is extremely fashionable and fairly affordable, Ratz takes a bizarre pride in his ugliness. His prosthesis is "grubby pink plastic" that looks like a "claw" (chap. 1). It jerks and whines. He sports a pot-belly, and the teeth in his mouth that are not steel are brown with decay. Instead of laughing, he grunts.

If, as in Phillipe Mora's 1982 film, the human form is a superficial lie that houses the beast within, then, in Gibson the rational human mind is a fragile veneer that tries to cover an insane core. Often that core breaks through the veneer. Not only does Armitage go mad, but so does Ashpool and the crowds at the Sense/Net Pyramid during their mass hallucination. There is ample evidence as well that Tessier, 3Jane, and Wintermute-Neuromancer are mentally unbalanced. Reason, Gibson posits, is a fine line away from unreason. The irrational may irrupt into everyday rationality at any time.

Even organized religion, a traditional emblem of community and stability, is seen as potentially crazed and possibly hazardous. Riding the trans-BAMA local, Case notices two "predatory-looking" Christian Scientists "edging toward" a trio of business women who look like "tall, exotic grazing animals" (chap. 5). Such a metaphor turns religion into a carnivore stalking its prey. The Panther

Moderns find commercialized high-tech religion a kind of bad joke, choosing to broadcast from a Sons-of-Christ-the-King satellite during their assault on Sense/Net. The implication is that one form of hallucination (television) can be used to create another (religion). Molly equates religious relics, like the left hand of John the Baptist at Topkapi, with the technological junk found in Finn's shop; significantly, the hand is kept in a museum that used to be a whorehouse for a king. The ludicrous Zionites live in an isolated and drugged universe of hydroponic ganja, mysticism, and sensuous music, virtually unaware of time, space, or free will. When Wintermute contacts them, they misconstrue its name as Winter Mute and believe it is a prophet announcing the Final Days. The Panther Moderns, Molly, and the Zionites equate religion (Sons of Christ the King, relics, false prophets) with technology (a satellite, junk in Finn's shop, Wintermute). Religion and technology, they seem to imply, are two different but similar discourses designed to order the world. People such as the Zionites employ the former. People such as Molly employ the latter. If this is true, then, technology becomes a kind of religion, religion a kind of technology. Neither is inherently superior to the other. Both are potentially unreliable, unexceptional, and potentially dangerous.

Gibson further upsets traditional distinctions between religion and technology by casting a mystical aura around machines. The result is a cybernetic sublime. In *A Philosophical Enquiry into the Origin of Our Ideas of the Sublime and the Beautiful* (1757), Edmund Burke argues against the neoclassical idea that the best art is rational and clear. Instead, he embraces the romantic notion that great art is that which touches upon the infinite. By definition, the infinite cannot be rational and clear. Moreover, the imagination is most intrigued and affected by art that is ambiguous, uncertain, and unclear, and by that which creates sensations of fear and astonishment. Burke calls this the sublime. Wintermute-Neuromancer embodies it. Throughout the novel Wintermute-Neuromancer remains ubiquitous, boundless, able to appear anywhere and touch anyone. It represents vast knowledge that cannot be known by humans. It appears by means of indistinct intimations, whispers, a voice speaking out of a babel of tongues. God-like, it manifests itself in various forms, once even offering to show itself as the burning bush from Exodus. In the matrix, Wintermute is represented as a cube of white light, "that very simplicity suggesting extreme complexity," its walls "seeth[ing] with faint internal shadows, as though a thousand dancers whirled behind a vast sheet of frosted glass" (chap. 9). Mesmerized, Case tries to approach and understand it. He cannot. Confronted by the cybernetic sublime, he flatlines for forty seconds.

The appearance of the cybernetic sublime is only one example of the larger infusion of the fantastic and fantasy elements into the science-fiction genre. Gibson continually imbues scenes with magic, often exploiting a dualistic or Todorovian epistemological stutter between the mimetic and the marvelous to disrupt conventional perception. Sometimes this takes the form of mild Pynchonesque background noise, as when Case picks up a beer in the Chat and "one of those strange instants of silence decended, as though a hundred unrelated conversations had simultaneously arrived at the same pause" (chap. 1). Sometimes a whole scene will reverberate with the unaccountable or astonishing, as when Lupus Yonderboy abruptly materializes out of nowhere and announces Wintermute's name to Case for the first time, or when Wintermute rings each phone in the airport once as Case passes. Sometimes Gibson launches a deliberate frontal assault on reason by presenting two mutually exclusive possibilities as correct: Case *both* flatlines, hence exhibiting no brain activity, *and* simultaneously dreams that he meets with Wintermute in the matrix, a process which would have to assume brain activity.

In addition to introducing this epistemological stutter into his text, Gibson also introduces various narrative tropes from the discursive universe of fantasy. Use of the magic word, for instance, plays a central role in the novel; Case, Molly, and the others are on a grail-quest for the word that will unite Wintermute and Neuromancer, and 3Jane holds the key. The story of cryogenics echoes the many stories of fairy-tale sleep. Sorcerers abound, from Wintermute-Neuromancer itself, to Riviera, who literally puts on a magic show.

Such use of the fantastic and fantasy elements interrogates traditional notions of reality, and underscores the tenuous quality of objectivity. Like Ovid, Gibson presents metamorphosis (of self, gender, psychological state, world, even universe of discourse) as the human condition. He thereby intimates nothing is constant, everything in a state of flux. Further, he apparently welcomes this existential situation. Not only does he thus challenge the norms of the conventional novel in general, but also of science fiction in particular. He disrupts the quasi-rational discourse of scientific extrapolation by charging it with the irrational and mystical discourse of the fantastic and fantasy. Consequently, he both invites readers to contemplate the future, and, as Rosemary Jackson says of the fantastic, "points to or suggests the basis upon which cultural order rests, [by] open[ing] up, for a brief moment, on to disorder, on to illegality, on to that which lies outside the law, that which is outside the dominant value systems."[15]

This might account for the numerous references to eyes throughout the novel. The reader obviously discovers the pervasive presence of Molly's mirrorshades. But he or she also comes across scenes where Riviera smashes one of Molly's lenses, Riviera blinds Hideo with his laser, and Molly poisons Riviera with a paralytic drug so that he will lose control of all his muscles but those in his eyes. Such emphasis on seeing and partial sight leads to the theme of relativistic perception. Humans, Gibson intimates, cannot partake in objective reality. They cannot see the whole picture of each other, the world, or themselves. Instead, they must learn, like the protagonist in "Fragments of a Hologram Rose," to accept subjective perception as the only kind available to them. At the level of narrative, this means that communal plot (public, objective, chronological, external, real) gives way to authorial plot (private, subjective, chronologically disjunctive, internal, imagined). At a metaphysical level, it means that normalcy is an illusion, a concept that depends upon a communally- accepted definition while the idea of the communal has already been deconstructed.

But the conclusion of the novel seems to belie the notion that ontological and epistemological normalcy is dangerous by its assertion of a narratologically "normal" ending. Following the conventions of a traditional nineteenth-century novel, *Neuromancer* finishes with several "marriages." Wintermute and Neuromancer "marry," becoming a single entity that dominates the matrix, and Wintermute-Neuromancer "marry" an AI in the Centauri system. Although Case loses Molly, he settles down with a woman named Michael in the Sprawl. And his construct settles down with Linda Lee in cyberspace. More, he is able to receive a new pancreas and liver, buy a new Ono-Sendai, and return home like the traditional heroic figure and characters in Renaissance comedy. In *Mona Lisa Overdrive*, the reader will learn that Case retires and has four children (chap. 22). The impression one takes away, then, might be one of symmetry, aesthetic harmony, and completeness. A novel conceived of as an "anti-*Star Wars* of SF"[16] seems finally to endorse a *Star Wars* sense of closure and readerly reassurance. A novel dedicated to ontological, epistemological, and narratological disruption seems finally to endorse communal ontology, epistemology, and narratology.

Yet this affirmative reading does not quite pan out. If one views *Neuromancer* through the textual lenses of *Count Zero* and *Mona Lisa Overdrive*, one soon realizes the apparent sense of harmony will be short-lived indeed. It is only a matter of time before Wintermute-Neuromancer comes apart like Slothrop at the end of *Gravity's Rainbow*, neither dying nor living, but simply scattering, "fragments of Slothrop hav[ing] grown into consistent personae of their own."[17] Wintermute-Neuromancer becomes a series of voodoo gods or subprograms. Although Case receives a new pancreas and liver, one is fairly sure he will damage those organs with drugs just as he did his original ones. Although he buys a new Ono-Sendai and returns to the Sprawl, it is unclear that he has learned anything important and lasting during his adventures; he briefly learns altruism when he heads in to Straylight to rescue Molly, but he almost immediately forgets his lesson. Rather than Ulysses heroically returning home to Ithaca, Case might simply and antiheroically be back where he started. While it is true the final image of the novel captures a happy trio in cyberspace, it is also true that that image is followed by the sound of Dixie Flatline's disconcerting and inhuman laughter which isn't laughter; it is as though cynical comedy undercuts stereotypical harmony (and there is the suggestion that Dixie Flatline's wish that his program be erased hasn't been honored). Finally, the last line of the novel, an echo of the one in Chandler's *The Big Sleep*, registers loss, not closure: "He never saw Molly again."[18] Case did not "marry" the character the reader might have expected him to marry, and the novel ends on a note of melancholy, not completeness. Further, that Gibson borrows directly from another author for his last line also generates a note of artifice at the very moment one might have expected sincerity.

So while *Neuromancer* might appear to belie its vision of cosmic flux with its seemingly conclusive conclusion, it in fact presents the reader with a complex and highly ambivalent ending in which harmony undercuts disharmony at the same time that disharmony disrupts harmony. Gibson once again posits two mutually exclusive possibilities as correct. This is a typically postmodern strategy. An attack upon reason, logic, and borders, Gibson's first novel postulates a situation that goes nowhere (and everywhere) while traveling at an astonishing velocity. It is comfortable with ontological, epistemological, and narrotological instability. It is comfortable with extreme indeterminacy. And, in the final analysis, it teaches that paradox and contradiction beat at the heart of the postmodern condition. For us to be survivors, we must learn to be like the amoral, insensitive, and quasi-autistic Case and Molly. We must learn to be twenty-first-century shockwave riders skimming the boiling crests of possibility, cultural schizophrenia, and visionary intensity.

Endnotes

[1] Larry McCaffery, "An Interview with William Gibson," *Mississippi Review* 16.2 & 3 (1988), 221.
[2] McCaffery, 225.
[3] Ibid., 225.
[4] Ibid., 222.
[5] Ibid., 225.
[6] The reader should always pay close attention to Gibson's choice of names for his characters, particularly in *Neuromancer*. Case is en*cased* in a shell that doesn't allow him to feel; Molly is an ex-"moll," or prostitute; "Armitage" suggests armor, armament, and even Armageddon; Linda Lee's name comes from the Velvet Underground's song, "Cool It Down"; and so on.
[7] David Porush, "Cybernauts in Cyberspace: William Gibson's *Neuromancer*," in *Aliens: The Anthropology of Science Fiction*, ed. George Slusser and Eric Rabkin (Carbondale: Southern Illinois UP, 1987), 171.
[8] Porush, 171.
[9] From a letter to me dated 27 July, 1989.
[1] Leanne C. Harper, "The Culture of Cyberspace," *The Bloomsbury Review* 8.5. (September/October 1988), 17.
[11] Joseph Nicholas and Judith Hanna, "William Gibson," *Interzone* 1.13 (1985), 17.
[12] Carol McGuirk, "The 'New' Romancers: Science Fiction Innovators from Gernsback to Gibson," paper delivered at the Fiction 2000 conference at the University of Leeds, June 28-July 1, 1989, 18.
[13] Samuel Delany, "Is Cyberpunk a Good Thing or a Bad Thing?" *Mississippi Review* 16.2 & 3 (1988), 32.
[14] This despite the fact that Gibson says he has not yet seen *Tron*.
[15] Rosemary Jackson, *Fantasy: The Literature of Subversion* (New York: Methuen, 1981), 4.
[16] Mikal Gilmore, "The Rise of Cyberpunk," *Rolling Stone* (December 4, 1986), 77.
[17] Thomas Pynchon, *Gravity's Rainbow* (New York: Viking, 1973), 742.
[18] A number of critics' observations notwithstanding, Gibson maintains this is an incorrect reading of the last line of the novel, which he added during galleys to close the movement of *N* in his own mind, thereby preventing a possible sequel. He says he has never read *The Big Sleep* and finds Chandler a boring author. For him the feeling generated by the last line should be be one of sadness, not artifice.

Count Zero

> Every bond you break
> Every step you take
> *I'll be watching you*
>   —Sting, "Every Breath You Take"

Gibson initially had no intention of writing a sequel to *Neuromancer*. Instead, he began entertaining a proposal he received to write a very different book set in a very different universe. In fact, he thought he had clinched the matter by making the last line of *Neuromancer* read that Case never saw Molly again. This, Gibson says, "was a deliberate move on my part to cut the cord right there."[1] Such a gesture would, he assumed, effectively prevent him from going back to his protagonists and hence to the Sprawl, and it would free him up to move in new directions.

But that isn't what happened. Influenced in part by the Hollywood world he now began to frequent and no doubt in part by the impressive critical and financial success of *Neuromancer*, Gibson began writing a second novel along the same lines as the first. This would ultimately become *Count Zero* (1986). To get around the problem of having to deal with Case and Molly's further exploits in any depth, he set his new work several years after *Neuromancer*, and peopled it with virtually all new characters, if not always new character types. Finn reappears briefly to make one or two offhand remarks about "this street samurai" he once knew who got a job working with "a Special Forces type" and a "cowboy they scraped up out of Chiba." Finn says he last saw them in Istanbul "seven, eight years" ago, and he heard the street samurai lived in London for a while after that (chap. 16). Although Molly, Armitage and Case are almost forgotten, much of the essential flavor of *Neuromancer* is not. Like Gibson's first novel, *Count Zero* evinces the by-now-familiar tough characters maneuvering at the fringes of a violent society filled with addictions and paranoid conspiracies. Like *Neuromancer*, it is epic or global in perspective, moving freely among such locations as the Sprawl, Arizona, Tennessee, Puerto Vallarta, Paris, Stockholm, and high orbit. Like *Neuromancer*, it involves a number of quests, including Turner's for his past, Marly Krushkhova's for the creator of the Cornell-like boxes, and Josef Virek's for immortality. And, like *Neuromancer*, it has the feel of a roller-coaster ride, providing the reader with a hook on every page.

Many familiar themes resurface as well, including the human-as-commodity, betrayal, and violation. Among the most important is that the human has become a techno-centaur. Like Case, Bobby Newmark is a computer cowboy who merges with and in part becomes a machine when he jacks into a cyberspace deck. Like many characters whom Molly noticed on Memory Lane, Turner wears a socket behind his left ear.

But Gibson has done more than simply repeat this theme in *Count Zero*. He has also radicalized it, carried it further than he had in *Neuromancer*. The technological fuses with the organic in a deeper way, crawling inside and uniting with it to the point that the two are virtually indistinguishable. An emblem of this is the "claw" the doctor uses to seal Bobby's chest after he has been attacked by a gang. The claw is both organic and inorganic. Wound on a spool, it looks like brown beaded tape. Unwound, it begins to writhe, "headless, each bead a body segment, each segment edged with pale shining legs" (chap. 9), a kind of centipede. When this centipede is applied to the wound and its nervous system extracted, its claws lock shut, forming a surgical zipper. Similarly, the biochips in Angie's head read on a scanner like a cancer. Fashioned out of organic cells, they function as a computer. Using them, subprograms or spirits in the matrix speak through Angie. Her brain has become indistinguishable from a cyberspace deck. It is not that the technological has been attached to the human; it is that the technological and the human have become one. Angie is the apotheosis of the techno-centaur, a highly complicated conscious automaton. To a slightly lesser degree, the same is true of a number of characters in *Count Zero*, from Turner who is compared to a machine (chap. 17) to Conroy whose "voice was flat and uninflected, as though he'd modeled it after a cheap voice chip" (chap. 1).

It is a short step from the theme of human-as-techno-centaur to the motif of the Frankenstein monster. Josef Virek, who represents "a type of parallel evolution" (chap. 15) to Tessier and Ashpool in *Neuromancer*, longs for immortality as did Victor Frankenstein. Ironically, Virek is both the mad inventor who manipulates others to attain his ends and the monster who is kept alive in a series of support vats in Stockholm. Moreover, the kind of life-extension he has chosen echoes Ashpool's cryogenics to the extent that it verges on a living hell. Like the mythological Tithonus, Virek has been granted seemingly eternal life without eternal youth. Another Frankenstein figure is Christopher Mitchell, the researcher at Maas Biolabs who has produced immortal hybrid cells that form the building blocks of a new technology. He transforms Angie into a kind of monster by planting the biochips in her brain. Angie literally becomes her father's creation. Both Turner and Bobby partake in the Frankenstein motif as well in that they are both reconstructed humans, brought back Lazarus-like from death. Turner is even built out of the body parts of other humans.

As in Gibson's earlier work, the theme of the techno-centaur and the Frankenstein motif give rise to themes of identity and selfhood. Gibson once more underscores his belief that both identity and selfhood are always near to unknowable and continually teetering on the verge of becoming something inhuman. A key image that reinforces this idea in *Count Zero* is that of mirrors. It proliferates, from Bobby's Indo-Javanese mirrored aviator glasses, to the mirror shards in several of the Cornell-like boxes, to the mirror-domed space helmet Marly carries into the Place. It suggests a relativity of perception, an inability to see beyond surface, and a fractured sense of indivduality. True identity is covered, like the Hosaka surgeon whose face is polite and alert, "a perfect corporate mask" (chap. 11), or the escape plane with its mimetic polycarbon coating that can take on the colors and configurations of its environment. Early in the novel, Bobby fails to recognize himself when he looks in the mirror after flatlining, and in many ways his story involves a quest for an adult identity. Whenever she confronts her ex-lover, Marly is afraid of losing her identity and becoming his object. Virek has multiple selves. As Paco, his AI servant, understands: "señor enjoys any number of means of manifestation" (chap. 15). If humans are seldom what they seem, then, the world is seldom what it seems. This is a lesson Bobby learns from Lucas, whose innocuous-looking cane houses razor-sharp brass splines. Again, Gibson presents Ovidian metamorphosis as the human condition.

At the same time that *Count Zero* shares much with Gibson's earlier work, however, it also marks a number of departures for him.

These occur at the levels of theme, characterization, narrative structure, and technique. One of the most interesting shifts in theme centers on Gibson's interrogation of mind/body dualism. If in his earlier stories and first novel he clearly tends to associate the body with a decadent *chronos* and the mind with a transcendent *kairos*, then in *Count Zero* he confuses the two realms and complicates his allegiances. Originally cyberspace was equated with personal and cultural memory in Gibson's mind, and the implication was often that personal and cultural memory could be liberating; now the very idea of memory causes Turner to vomit (chap. 1). While Bobby's cyberspace deck still leads out of the "meat" world and into a dazzlingly imaginative realm, other gateways out of the "meat" world are hardly as appealing. Bobby's holoporn unit, for instance, seems "dated and vaguely ridiculous" (chap. 6). The biosoft containing Mitchell's dossier is less a window to a hyper-reality for Turner than one to vertigo and nausea. Marly realizes that "the sinister thing about a simstim construct, really, was that it carried the suggestion that *any* environment might be unreal. . . . Mirrors, someone had once said, were in some way essentially unwholesome; constructs were more so, she decided" (chap. 18). More than enough evidence for this can be found in Bobby's mother's addiction to her soap operas with their multiheaded plots that curl into themselves like tapeworms. If the television, video games, and Walkmans that formed the basis for cyberspace once held fascination and the possibility of postmodern joy for Gibson, they now hold disorientation and the possibility of evil. Gibson's attitude toward high-tech mass media, then, has become increasingly ambivalent. This tendency will become more pronounced in *Mona Lisa Overdrive*, where it is clear Gibson has become jaded and frazzled by the Westcoast cosmos he began to sample after the publication of *Neuromancer*.

In addition to this shift at the level of theme in *Count Zero*, there is also a marked shift at the level of characterization. In Gibson's first novel, characters have next to no personal past and little psychological depth. By way of example, one might think of Case. The reader knows virtually nothing of his existence previous to the events depicted in *Neuromancer* aside from the fact that he once double-crossed his former boss and was punished for his impudence. The reader is seldom privy to his thoughts and learns that Case feels next to nothing, that he has been numb to the world for years. He cannot love and he cannot hate. In contrast, one discovers something much closer to traditional characterization in *Count Zero*. Not only does the reader have a sense of Turner's professional background but also of his personal history. The reader knows of Turner's mother's long lonely death by cancer, sees and feels his prodigal return home and his wordless struggle with himself and with his brother about the responsibility he refused to accept during family crisis. The reader even shares several of Turner's childhood memories, including those that recall his edenic days squirrel hunting with his brother. Turner's love for his child is evident in the last chapter of the novel, as is his growing parental protectiveness of Angie throughout. Such use of public and private flashbacks, psychological density, and evidence of human feeling results in a greater emotional texture to the narrative than that found in *Neuromancer* or *Burning Chrome*.

Several shifts occur in narrative structure and technique as well. While Gibson informs Turner's story with the gangster-heist plot borrowed from the realm of pop fiction and film, he also adds two new major structures borrowed from traditional mainstream literature. First, in the case of Marly and Alain, Gibson adopts the plot from the nineteenth-century realist novel that maps love and betrayal. Second, in the case of Bobby, he adopts the plot from the nineteenth-century *Erziehungsroman*, or novel of education, that tracks a character's development as he or she passes from childhood into adulthood, in the process discovering his or her identity and role in society. At the same time that Gibson employs more conventional plotlines, he also paradoxically employs greater technical disruption. Like Pynchon, he begins using an unusually large and sometimes bewildering cast of characters and, the novel's title notwithstanding, he does not focus on a clear protagonist. Rather, he makes use of three main characters (Turner, Marly, Bobby) whose plotlines slowly dovetail as the novel unfolds. Each of the thirty-six chapters is located primarily within the point-of-view of one of these characters so that, as in a text like Faulkner's *As I Lay Dying*, emphasis falls on the relativity of perception. Turner, Marly, and Bobby, privy to different realms of experience, often read the same event differently from each other. The reader is thus reminded once again of Gibson's seed-story, "Fragments of a Hologram Rose." To lend Gibson's text meaning, the reader must become Faulkner's fourteenth blackbird, the one that pulls all the other fragments together into a mosaic which to a large degree is no more than simply one approximation of "truth."

Of the three highly complex and often confusing plotlines, Turner's is most well-known to readers of Gibson. Typically, Gibson both adopts and transforms the gangster-heist story in the twelve chapters dedicated to Turner. As in *Neuromancer*, mercenaries are hired as part of an elite team whose mission is to steal something of great value. Whereas in Gibson's first novel the loot is an artificial intelligence, here it is a human being. Turner believes his job is to extract Christopher Mitchell, a top research scientist responsible for the development of biochips, from his home of nine years in Maas Biolabs North America and bring him over to a Hosaka compound in Mexico City. Conroy, Turner's boss, flies Turner to an off-shore oil rig where he meets part of his nine-person team. Turner then continues on to Arizona to complete preparations at a site near Biolabs' mesatop research arcology.

Here the mission runs into a snag. Mitchell allows his daughter Angie to escape in his place, then commits suicide. While Turner and his people scramble to retrieve Angie from the debris of the ultralight she used to escape the arcology, they come under attack by unknown assailants. Turner and Angie have just enough time to take off in a jet before the site and its remaining inhabitants are destroyed by a hypervelocity gun. Unsure of where to go, Turner heads to his parents' home in Tennessee where he meets Rudy, his brother, and Rudy's lover, Sally. Rudy runs tests on Angie and discovers Mitchell has grafted biochips onto her brain. Through them, subprograms or spirits from the matrix communicate with her. Guided by these, Angie leads Turner to Bobby Newmark, whose handle is Count Zero, at a club in the Sprawl run by a man named Jammer.

At this club, pieces begin to fall together. Turner learns that in graduate school Mitchell realized he would never be as brilliant as he needed to be in order to rise to the heights of the corporate ladder. Faust-like, he cut a deal with one or more of the subprograms or spirits in cyberspace. Mitchell received information that led to the discovery of the biochips, while the subprograms or spirits received Angie's mind and body. Furthermore, Turner learns that Conroy has been acting as a double-agent. Ostensibly, Conroy extracted Mitchell for Hosaka. In fact, he did so for Josef Virek, a mysterious and wealthy art collector reminiscent of Howard Hughes. It was Conroy, Turner finds, who attacked the extraction site in order to kill the Hosaka team. It also comes to light that Conroy tortured Turner's brother to death in order to find out where Turner and Angie have gone. With this information in hand, Bobby alerts Jaylene Slide, a computer hacker whose lover Conroy murdered when attacking the extraction site. As revenge, Jaylene Slide kills Conroy. Angie leaves with Beauvoir, an *oungan* or voodoo priest of cyberspace who will teach her the ways of the matrix. Turner decides to return to his Tennessee home, retire, and raise a child with Sally.

Because Turner's plotline is most well-known to readers of Gibson, only three points about it need to be underscored here. First, through this plot Gibson emphasizes the near-future shift in global power from state to corporation. He suggests that the idea of boundaries between countries has begun to erode. The notion of government control has come to seem, like Bobby's holoporn deck, dated and vaguely ridiculous. This accounts for why the United States is never referred to by name in Gibson's works. The powerbase has been relocated in the multinationals that govern the flow of information, and hence capital and strength. Instead of defecting from one country to another, people like Mitchell now defect from one company to another. Instead of wars breaking out between country and country, they now break out between corporation and corporation. Angie even thinks of the multinational in the same terms others might once have thought about nations or religions. When Turner explains to her that Rudy is an unhappy alcoholic, she innocently asks if that is because he does not have a company to take care of him.

Second, while the conclusion of *Neuromancer* is potentially inconclusive and fairly unstable, the conclusion of Turner's plotline and *Count Zero* as a whole is potentially sentimental and virtually closed. Paul Alkon comments that Turner "retire[s] to the pastoral delights of the countryside where his days are agreeably occupied in hunting nothing more dangerous than squirrels."[2] Turner literally withdraws from the dystopic universe of the Sprawl, stepping back into an edenic one that connotes nostalgia, peace, and simplicity. Like Case who returns to the Sprawl, buys a new cyberspace deck, and settles down with a woman named Michael at the end of *Neuromancer*, Turner also becomes a Ulysses figure at the end of *Count Zero*. Integration follows on the heels of separation and education. Marly's and Bobby's plots will end at least as conventionally. Marly reaches the goal of her quest, discovering the artist behind the Cornell-like boxes and freeing herself from both Alain's and Virek's control. She also becomes operator of one of the most fashionable galleries in Paris. Bobby becomes Angie's lover and is paid for his efforts. The reader last views this couple two years after the main action of the novel has transpired. They are on location in Turkey, Angie having become simstim star Tally Isham's understudy. It is sunset. Angie, who has been lying naked on a rooftop, rises and takes Bobby's hand while Tally and her director look on enviously. "If this is not quite riding off into the sunset together," Alkon notes, "it is close enough to be recognized as a pleasant urban variation on that familiar sentimental ending."[3] Consequently, each of the plotlines concludes with either financial or personal success. Marly's and Bobby's end with both. And each of the plotlines concludes with a feeling of harmony, hope, and completion. While the bulk of each occurs in a dystopia, the end of each is something close to utopic.

A third point that should be underscored about Turner's plotline is that through Angie it introduces the reader to the flashy universe of high-tech mass media that will inform the central plotline of *Mona Lisa Overdrive*. Gibson's suspicion of this universe is evident in the last scene involving Angie. Tally and the director, emblems of this universe, literally *look down* upon Angie and Bobby from their balcony. They are poised like cormorants inspecting their unsuspecting prey who, like Adam and Eve in Milton's *Paradise Lost*, unwittingly prepare to abandon their edenic world for one that is permeated by danger, potential betrayal, and here ruthless social Darwinism. By looking forward to Angie's education about a world where art is a business and where business can be deadly, this scene foreshadows elements of the *Erziehungsroman* that will play a major role in shaping *Mona Lisa Overdrive*.

This theme of art-as-business leads directly into a consideration of *Count Zero*'s second major plotline. Also twelve chapters in length, this plotline focuses on Marly Krushkhova's quest for the originator of the Cornell-like boxes. Shortly after she is disgraced in the art world for unknowingly attempting to sell a Cornell forgery supplied by Alain, Marly is approached by Virek. Marly thinks she is working in the interests of art. The truth is that the ailing Virek is using her for his own egoistic ends. He believes the originator of the boxes is in a position to offer him freedom from his support vat. When Marly meets with Alain to discover where he found the forgery, he demands money for the information. Marly agrees to pay him, but when she shows up at his apartment with the cash, she finds him murdered. She searches his apartment for clues and discovers an address that leads her into high orbit, to part of the Tessier-Ashpool cores housing their mainframes. She learns that, shortly after the events described in *Neuromancer*, 3Jane entered financial difficulty, sold out, and had Straylight detached from Freeside and towed to a new orbit. The cores were supposedly erased and sold to a scrapper who never salvaged the expensive metals within them. In the cores, Marly meets Wigan Ludgate, a mad religious fanatic, and his henchman Jones. Jones leads her to the originator of the boxes: a manipulator or robot connected to what is left of the Tessier-Ashpool computers — to what is left, in other words, of Wintermute and Neuromancer. Marly finds out that, like Tessier before him, Virek imagines he can encode his personality into the mainframes and thereby gain immortality and omnipotence. But his plan fails. He overextends his power trying to keep Angie, who he believes might have information that will help him in his endeavor, trapped at Jammer's club. Weakened, he is attacked by the subprograms or spirits in the matrix and is killed. Paco, Virek's servant, appears on the screen and tells Marly she is now free.

A pathetic image of the artist, the robot that constructs the boxes registers a new portrayal of the creator on Gibson's part. This emotionless sculptor works in isolation, oblivious to the humans who move around it. Quasi-autistic, it mechanically generates junkboxes that produce strong feelings solely in others. On one level, it is emblematic of the postmodern *gomi no sensei*. To this extent it looks back to Rubin Stark in "The Winter Market" and ahead to Slick Henry in *Mona Lisa Overdrive*. It is thereby also emblematic of Gibson himself. Embodied in it is an image of the man who views himself as a collage-artist constructing verbal sculptures from the detritus of our culture.

Gibson consequently links the image of himself as a creator with that of Joseph Cornell (1903-1972), the original creator of the junk-boxes. An American artist of the irrational, Cornell was a recluse who avoided dealers, collectors, and critics. He admired Stéphane Mallarmé and the French Symbolists, who in turn admired Edgar Alan Poe whose gothic sense of mystery and imagination pervades Gibson's work. Cornell crammed his house on Utopia Parkway in Queens, New York, with old photos, books, and cartons filled with cultural waste. During the 1930's, he began assembling collages that imitated those of Max Ernst, and soon began experimenting with his signature creations that fused the illusionary quality of surrealist paintings with the concreteness of Dadaist found objects. Reminiscent of cluttered Straylight, these boxes, housing everything from watchsprings to fossils, gems to cork balls, suggest at least three ideas that appeal to Gibson. First, they resemble specimen cases; this image points to the notion of the artist as a kind of scientist, an archeologist of the present, exploring the details of his or her society and recording them for future generations. Second, the boxes conjure up pictures of tiny stages, and thus of the theatre; this image gives rise to themes having to do with appearance versus reality, artifice, and identity — all of which play important roles in Gibson's fiction. Third, the boxes remind one of Victorian mementos; this image, grounded in the historical period Gibson most often mentions, carries with it a certain nostalgic charge and consideration of the past that will become increasingly pronounced in Gibson's work.

Unlike other artist figures in Gibson's short stories and novels, however, the robot in the Tessier-Ashpool cores creates *fake* art. It creates simulacra of Cornell boxes, not the boxes themselves. And it apparently feels next to nothing during the act of creation. Something, in other words, has gone out of the creative process which has become involuntary, automatic, perfunctory. While others might experience intense emotion from the result of this lifeless process of replication, the artist experiences nothing. Art has gone moribund. It is now mass-produced by a machine, having become no more than a product one manufactures so that others such as Alain might benefit financially. And those who do benefit financially from it are portrayed as amoral criminals. This also leads the reader back to "The Winter Market," written immediately after

Count Zero. While there are a number of differences between story and novel, both Lise and the robot are literally shut off from others; the former is locked within her polycarbon exoskeleton, the latter within the Tessier-Ashpool cores. Both are self-absorbed. And both are used by others, the former by the simstim industry that allows Lise to become addicted to wizz, the latter by everyone from Ludgate to Virek.

No one except Marly in *Count Zero* thinks of art in any but monetary terms. Picard, manager of The Roberts Gallery in Paris, for instance, seldom sees the art he purchases. Rather, it is crated and stored in a vault until he orders it sold, convinced that its stock has risen sufficiently to make it financially worthwhile. Andrea, Marly's friend, understands that people like Alain are "artists in their own right," but only to the extent that they are "intent on restructuring reality" (chap. 10) — on lying in order to generate capital. It comes as no surprise that Alain is a forger by trade. An icon of this world, he deals in false art designed to make money. The price paid by such "artists" is their humanity. An example of this may be found in the story Turner recalls about Jane Hamilton, the simstim actress for whom Turner once provided security in Mexico. Despite Turner's efforts, Hamilton is assassinated. Almost immediately a Sense/Net carrier shows up, not in order to investigate the murder or to reclaim Hamilton's body, but to repossess her artificial Zeiss Ikon eyes that are worth several million New Yen. The human is easily forgotten; finances are not.

Sense/Net, Virek, Maas Biolabs, Hosaka, and those other ubiquitous malignant forces that control this megacorporate universe once again take on the omniscient and omnipotent proportions of Pynchon's elect. Appropriately, then, the first word of this novel is a megalithic, anonymous and deadly *They*. If in *Neuromancer* Case understands that the dominant image of the megacorporation is the wasp nest, here Marly understands it is the "intricate machine." She realizes she is a tool in Virek's hands, part of "a machine so large that I am incapable of seeing it. A machine that surrounds me, anticipating my every step" (chap. 12). Essentially demonic, this machine divides, multiplies, and operates across national boundaries. Virek, Tessier-Ashpool, and the others who keep the machine in motion are "no longer even remotely human" (chap. 2). They are capable of anything to insure a profit. Moreover, individuals easily become addicted to their roles as tools for the machine. A medic at the extraction site in Arizona explains that corporations now equip employees with subdermals that trick the employee's system into a reliance on certain synthetic enzyme analogs; withdrawal from the employer results in trauma. Metaphorically, people learn to depend upon the machine for a feeling of comfort, security, and order. For many, the machine provides the external structure they need to survive.

Mere tools, humans function with only an illusion of free will. During his recovery in Puerto Vallarta, for example, Turner has an affair with a woman named Allison whom he believes he has met by chance. She turns out to be a "field psychologist" paid to oversee his convalescence. After Virek hires her, Marly chooses a hotel at random, but a package from Virek mysteriously finds her there. Virek, she discovers, continually knows where she will be and when. Later, he explains that he has run a psychoprofile on her that has predicted each of her responses. Although she wants to believe she has been acting spontaneously, she has actually been carrying out the machine's will.

Given her relationship to the corporate elect, Marly has much in common with Oedipa Maas in Pynchon's *The Crying of Lot 49*. Both women sense levels of reality beyond their comprehension, yet cannot determine exactly what those levels consist of. Both move from a safe predictable universe into a dangerous unpredictable one, from a naive vision of the world into a dark labyrinthian plot that signals education. For Oedipa, the minotaur is Pierce Inverarity, whose name suggests inveracity. For Marly, whose name suggests the mirror image of tough Molly, the minotaur is Josef Virek. Both are controlled by powerful individuals who haunt them from beyond the grave. Both are victims of men. Oedipa not only explores a *mail* system in her quest, but also a *male* system. Likewise, Marly explores the intricate machine and learns it is dominated by males. From her perspective, it is governed by Alain who uses her by foisting a forgery into her hands, and by Virek who uses her by lying about the goal of her mission. She discovers, as will a number of characters in *Mona Lisa Overdrive*, a patriarchal network wherein one's movements have already to a certain degree been predetermined by conventions of gender. Unlike *The Crying of Lot 49*, however, *Count Zero* offers an alternative to this situation. The novel provides several strong women who do not find themselves trapped by the patriarchal network. There is the lesbian, Webber, for instance, the hard-boiled Molly-like figure at the extraction site, and Rez, the pilot of the space tug who transports Marly to the Tessier-Ashpool cores. More important, Oedipa ultimately fails in her quest to find who is behind the WASTE system while Marly succeeds. She is freed (albeit by chance rather than by significant action on her part) from both Alain's and Virek's control. The implication is that there is at least some degree of hope for liberation from the male system — if not, finally, from the intricate machine itself.

If Marly's plotline involves her education about the monetary nature of the corporate elect, then, Bobby Newmark's involves his education about the spiritual nature of the cyberspace matrix. Again twelve chapters in length, this third major plotline in *Count Zero* focuses on a fledgling hacker who lives with his mother in Barrytown, New Jersey. He rents an icebreaker from a software dealer named Two-a-Day and flatlines almost immediately upon trying to use it. He is saved by Angie's presence that appears to him in the matrix as Vyéj Mirak, voodoo goddess of miracles, and he goes in search of Two-a-Day to find out what happened, only to be mugged and robbed of his icebreaker on the way. Two-a-Day locates and repairs him, then informs him that he has used Bobby as a guinea pig to discover what the icebreaker does. He also tells Bobby that he got it from two oungans, Beauvoir and Lucas. They in turn got it from Finn, who in turn got it from Wigan Ludgate, the mad religious fanatic living in the Tessier-Ashpool cores. Accompanied by one of Lucas's henchmen, Bobby heads to Jammer's club for safe keeping. Once there, two street gangs show up to make sure no one can leave. Bobby jacks into Jammer's cyberspace deck to trace who is behind the gangs, and meets Jaylene Slide, Conroy's data rustler, searching for her lover's murderer. While Bobby is jacked in, Turner and Angie appear. Turner learns about Conroy's betrayal and tells Bobby, who in turn tells Jaylene. Jaylene kills Conroy just as he is assuring Virek that he will bring Angie to him the next day. Bobby also witnesses the beginning of Virek's demise in the matrix. Having now become a Ulysses-figure like Case in *Neuromancer*, Bobby jacks out to discover that his mother, whom he thought murdered in an attack on his condo, is alive. Nonetheless, he decides to leave his life with her, and accompany Angie and Beauvoir back to Beauvoir's place in Barrytown to learn ways of the loa, or voodoo spirits, that have begun inhabiting the matrix. Two years later, Bobby turns up as Angie's companion on location in Turkey.

Most significant about this plotline is its introduction of loa into the matrix. At the moment Neuromancer and Wintermute merge at the end of Gibson's first novel, becoming a god-like unity of opposites, the newly generated entity fragments. This is partially because this entity is lonely, partially because it wants to have some fun, and partially, as the reader learns in *Mona Lisa Overdrive*, for unknown reasons having to do with a similar artificial intelligence on Centauri. The fragmentation produces a host of smaller gods in the matrix that adopt names of voodoo deities. Wigan Ludgate, one of the first to intuit the spiritual dimension of cyberspace, begins worshipping these deities from his high orbit home in the Tessier-Ashpool cores. Oungans such as Beauvoir and Lucas do the same on earth. They thereby assume the role of wizards in fantasy, educating acolytes like Bobby in the mystical ways of the loa. Unlike the virtuous saints, angels, and other religious beings that form traditional Christianity, however, these voodoo deities are filled with street-savvy, lust, and greed. Unpredictable and potentially harmful, they are descendents of pagan gods and goddesses.

A large part of the idea for them came from Carole Devillers' *National Geographic* article, "Haiti's Voodoo Pilgrimages: Of Spirits and Saints," which Gibson read while working on *Count Zero*.[4] In this piece, Devillers gives a brief account of voodoo beliefs, gods, and celebrations. Gibson found at least four of its basic ideas appealing. First, he registered the fact that voodoo is a hybrid religion that blends two faiths. The Creole name for voodoo is *vodou*, which in turn comes from *vodun*, a word that means *spirit* in the language of the Fon people of Benin and Nigeria. Brought to Haiti as slaves by the French in the seventeenth century, these West Africans were forbidden to practice their ancestral religion and were pressured into converting to Roman Catholicism. In the process, they merged components of their traditional religion with components of the European one. The result was a third religion in which ancestral spirits took on the names of Catholic saints. Part of the role of this religion's oungan, or priest, is to "serve with both hands," to practice black magic as well as voodoo. Appropriate to Gibson's world, voodoo is both a spiritual collage and an originally outlaw-religion created by those whom the dominant society marginalized. While Gibson satirizes conventional religion by identifying it in this novel with Bobby's crazed mother, he treats voodoo with greater seriousness, implying that it has roots in opposition and exists, at least in its Hollywood stereotypes, in a dark realm of potential danger, mystery, and intrigue. It is, according to Beauvoir, a "*street* religion" that "came out of a dirt-poor place" (chap. 13). Moreover, the idea of overlaying one universe of discourse (African ancestoral religion) upon another (Roman Catholicism) suggests the same kind of multiplicity of meaning Gibson achieves when he overlays the language of technology (subprograms) upon the language of religion (loa). Like the voodoo oungans, Gibson's text serves with both hands.

Second, Gibson found voodoo's notion of god appropriate to a computer society. According to African-Haitian belief, god is *Gran Mèt*, or the great maker of Heaven and Earth. But, as Beauvoir puts it, this god is "too big and too far away to worry Himself if your ass is poor, or you can't get laid" (chap. 13). Too powerful and important to concern himself directly with mere human beings, he sends down his loa to possess and communicate with them. The voodooist must consult with these loa before embarking on any serious activity. Often the loa will "ride" an individual without warning, sending him or her into dance, trance, or song. And often this takes place at a *lieu saint*, or holy place, such as among a stand of trees that are considered natural temples. In Gibson's world, Neuromancer-Wintermute is literally remote from humans, buried within the Tessier-Ashpool cores in high orbit. Only Wigan Ludgate feels its presence in any profound way. Its loa, however, exist in the matrix on earth and do deals with the likes of Beauvoir, Lucas, and Mitchell. They ride Angie. And they are associated with Two-a-Day, whose place is filled with trees, from his driftwood coffee table to his stunted forest raised on "gro-lights."

Third, Gibson felt that voodoo's minimalization of afterlife jibed well with postmodern existence. According to Beauvoir, "it isn't concerned with notions of salvation and transcendence. What it's about is getting things *done*" (chap. 13). This takes the reader back to the question of human-as-conscious-automaton that Gibson explored in his first novel. Action in Gibson's world precedes essence. Thinking and feeling, as Molly knows so well, are secondary to doing.

Finally, Gibson loved the poetry of the words associated with voodoo beliefs, gods, and celebrations, and he uses them frequently in *Count Zero* and *Mona Lisa Overdrive* for sound as much as for sense. While references abound to such loa as Danbala Wedo (the snake), Ougou Feray (spirit of war), and Baron Samedi (lord of the graveyards), perhaps most important are Legba and Ezili Freda. Appropriately enough for a novel about computers, the former is the loa of communications and is associated with Bobby, the console cowboy. Legba is identified with St. Peter, Christian doorkeeper of heaven, and in voodoo rituals must always be invoked first; if not, the other loa might not listen. The latter, also known as Vyéj Mirak, or Our Lady Virgin of Miracles, is the loa of love and is associated with Angie, who protects others from evil. Ezili Freda is identified with the Virgin Mary, mother of Christ who shelters the penitent.

From one perspective, Gibson raises voodoo to the level of a grand art by basking in its poetic language. From a slightly different perspective, he neutralizes its power by suggesting that it is *no more* than grand art, poetic language; it is, in other words, simply a fiction, one way among others for organizing the world. Voodoo becomes a construct through which to describe an event. To this extent Beauvoir is correct when he asserts that voodoo is "just a *structure*." (chap. 13). Technology is an equally valid construct through which to describe the same event. Again, Gibson points to religion and technology as no more than language games, abstract organizations of data. Perhaps the gods in the matrix are real, as Beauvoir and Lucas believe. Perhaps they are no more than virus programs that have gotten loose in the matrix and replicated, as Jammer has it. Perhaps both possibilities are true simultaneously. If so, the reader is back to the question of a dualistic or Todorovian perspective. From one angle, the events in the matrix can be explained using the language of science. From another angle, only the language of the transcendental will do. Both languages are correct. Both languages are incorrect.

The result is a narratological, epistemological, and ontological stutter that once more focuses one's attention on the presence of postmodern fantasy in Gibson's work. Finn reminds the reader: "Yeah, there's things out there. Ghosts, voices. Why not? Oceans had mermaids, all that shit, and we had a sea of silicon, see?" (chap. 16). Alkon interprets: "First meditatively suggesting the possibility that real spirits of some eminence in the divine hierarchy may have arrived to haunt cyberspace, Finn then switches gears to suggest that such things are as fabulous as mermaids, and like them nothing more than fantasies projecting strange aspects of the human psyche into reports of *terra incognita*."[5] Gibson hence plays one mode of discourse (spiritual) off another (scientific), creating a dialectic that refuses synthesis and thus generates textual instability. Consequently, he produces readerly anxiety and doubt. He subverts and deforms traditional notions of narratology, ontology, and epistemology, announcing that at the center of postmodern existence pulses a deconstructive turn, a radical skepticism that embraces paradox and indeterminacy, suspicion and contradiction. Answer gives way to question. Totality gives way to multiplicity. The mimetic gravity of earth gives way to the magical weightlessness of the Tessier-Ashpool cores.

Endnotes

[1] Leanne C. Harper, "The Culture of Cyberspace," *The Bloomsbury Review* 8.5. (September/October 1988), 30.

[2] Paul Alkon, "Deus Ex Machina in William Gibson's Cyberpunk Trilogy," paper delivered at the Fiction 2000 conference at the University of Leeds, June 28-July 1, 1989, 4.

[3] Alkon, 5.

[4] Carole Devillers, "Haiti's Voodoo Pilgrimages: Of Spirits and Saints," *National Geographic* March 1985, 395-410. See also Robert Tallant, *Voodoo In New Orleans* (New York, Collier, 1962), originally published in 1946, which Gibson read as a teenager in Virginia; the *vevés* looked to him like circuit diagrams.

[5] Alkon, 15-16.

Mona Lisa Overdrive

Just wait till the Kid grows up.
—Bruce Sterling, *The Artificial Kid*

At one point in *Mona Lisa Overdrive* (1988), Angie's leading man tells her that an artificial intelligence named Continuity is writing a book. When Angie asks what the book is about, the leading man explains that it "looped back into itself and constantly mutated; Continuity was *always* writing it." Angie asks why. "Because," she is told, "Continuity was an AI, and AIs did things like that" (chap. 7). This serves nicely as a gloss on Gibson's own attempt to conclude the Matrix Trilogy. The artificial intelligence, aptly called Continuity, suggests Gibson himself whose tremendously complex plotline involving Wintermute, Neuromancer, and their offspring has constantly turned back into itself and mutated throughout the course of his short stories and novels. To this extent, Continuity is simply one more artist figure in a fiction filled with them. Interestingly, there is also an edge of weariness, even frustration, present in the statement: Continuity, after all, is *always* writing because that's what AI's *must* do. If in *Count Zero* the artist has become an isolated mechanical manipulator endlessly generating junk-boxes, here the artist has become an artificial intelligence writing out of necessity rather than desire. The result of that writing might be technically efficient, but it might also be relatively colorless.

Certainly this was the perception of many readers commenting on Gibson's least critically successful novel. In one of the book's most negative reviews, Paul Kincaid notes that "Gibson wrote one book of stunning originality which caught the mood of the time so successfully that he has been condemned to repeat it. By this third volume he is showing clear and dramatic improvement as a writer, but is doing nothing fresh with his talent."[1] There are at least four reasons to account for this sense of a falling off on Gibson's part. First, the reader spends less time in cyberspace here than he or she did in Gibson's earlier works, and the time he or she does spend in it is far less dazzling and surreal than before; yet cyberspace is perhaps the most original and captivating element of the Trilogy's geography. Second, there are virtually no new ideas or themes in *Mona Lisa Overdrive*; the reader has covered most of this terrain before. Third, for all of Gibson's concentration on characterization in *Mona Lisa Overdrive*, Kumiko Yanaka, Gibson's first fictional child, and a key figure in the novel, remains unconvincing to many. Fourth, despite his problems with conventional characterization, Gibson has continued his narratological move toward relatively more traditional story and discourse.

All four of these reasons might stem from the pressures exerted on him by the L.A. world with which he has become increasingly familiar. In interviews, he often makes the connection between beginning to work in Hollywood and beginning to write more about the intricate machine of Sense/Net. While he claims *Mona Lisa Overdrive* is "not autobiographical in any sense," he still admits that "there's a lot of the background for the Sense/Net stuff drawn from contemporary media life, and I simply wouldn't have had that material before [being exposed to Hollywood]."[2]

Set seven years after the central events of his last novel, *Mona Lisa Overdrive* is composed of forty-five chapters involving four intersecting plotlines. The first of these, containing thirteen chapters, focuses on Kumiko's rite of passage from childhood innocence to adulthood understanding. The basic plot structure takes the form of an *Erziehungsroman*. Kumi, daughter of a Japanese gangster, is sent to London on the eve of her thirteenth birthday to be housed and protected by Roger Swain, her father's subordinate, because of infighting among the Yakuza in Japan. There she learns someone is paying off Swain, who in turn is blackmailing Molly, to kidnap Angela Mitchell while making it appear as though she has been killed by supplying the body of a double. As events unfold, however, a twist occurs. Angie will be murdered and her double will replace her. Molly will also be killed. The person behind this conspiracy turns out to be an insane 3Jane. She wants Angie dead because she is jealous of her for having once come close to attaining a central position in the matrix through her biochip implants. 3Jane wants Molly dead to avenge her father's murder. Swain is eliminated for having gotten greedy with the information 3Jane began feeding him as payoff. Kumi is reunited with her father.

Kumi's education, like that of Marly in *Count Zero*, involves her exposure to the complex and deadly workings of a patriarchal system. With Molly as guide, Kumi learns to navigate among fathers, from her genetic one in Japan to her surrogates in London (Swain,

Petal, Tick). She also discovers that women like her mother and 3Jane who attempt to struggle against the dominant order suffer awful ends. From her point of view, only Molly, who learns to abandon this invisible male hierarchy completely in her retirement, survives. Through Molly there is again at least some degree of hope for liberation from the male system. But, as in Gibson's earlier works, there is virtually no hope for liberation from the intricate machine of the megacorporate elect. While Molly appears to strike off on her own at the conclusion of the novel, accompanied solely by a robot and the aleph, she is in a way still employed by the loa or subprograms to guard the personality constructs that the aleph houses. In other plotlines, Angie and Mona aren't so lucky. The megacorporate elect kills the former and reshapes the latter's identity to meet its needs, transforming both women into conscious automata with only illusions of free will.

Kumi's plotline also points to another major theme in the novel: the importance of the past. In *Count Zero*, Gibson began paying increasing attention to the presence and power of history in his characters' lives, carefully sketching in facts about Turner's childhood, his mother's death by cancer, and so on. Here, memory plays an even more pronounced role. Literal ghosts proliferate *Mona Lisa Overdrive*, from Kumi's mother to personality constructs such as Finn, Colin, and those of the previous Yakuza bosses kept by Kumi's father; these are emblems of memory that the characters cannot escape. If Japan stands for the future, then England, a dominant setting, stands for the past. While Tokyo nurtures what little history remains to it "with a nervous care," London celebrates history, a city where the past forms "the very fabric of things" (chap. 1). Angie tries to deny her past by throwing her father's biosoft dossier into the sea, but ultimately learns that she must literally live within history in the aleph. Slick Henry, whose short-term memory has been damaged by a technique administered while he was in prison, comes to realize how truly horrible the loss of history can be. Kumi discovers she must make peace with her past, with her mother's death and her father's possible role in it, to become a fully integrated personality. She understands that she is composed of her past and that she must learn to value it and deal with it.

Bobby Newmark comes to understand much the same in the course of his twelve chapters. His education takes place primarily at Thomas Trail Gentry's and Slick Henry's Factory in Dog Solitude. Shortly after the events that transpired in *Count Zero*, Bobby broke up with Angie and appeared in Mexico City with a neuroelectronic addiction. He obtained the aleph, a huge biochip with virtually unlimited storage capacity, from 3Jane who gave it to him to get in touch with the loa or subprograms that have begun fading in the matrix. 3Jane, in a bid for immortality similar to that of her mother's, used most of her family's wealth to build the aleph. Upon completion, she put her personality construct inside it and died. A petty thief delivers Bobby to Dog Solitude jacked into the aleph. He asks Gentry and Slick to watch him. Gentry, a computer cowboy in search of the overall shape of the matrix, becomes interested in Bobby and the aleph because he believes the latter might provide the grail for which he has been questing. Mercenaries representing 3Jane's interests attack the Factory in an attempt to retrieve the aleph. In the midst of the ensuing battle, Molly appears with Mona and Angie, saying she has made a deal with the loa or subprograms to get Angie and Bobby together in the aleph. In return, the loa or subprograms will cause her criminal record to be erased. Angie's construct enters the aleph after her death. Slick, an artist who produces huge robots, sets up one of these called the Judge to carry the aleph for Molly, who sets out alone across Dog Solitude.

Bobby has come closer than anyone in the Matrix Trilogy to voluntarily leaving the "meat" world behind and entering the pure realm of the mind. Existing almost solely within the aleph, he pays little attention to his body, which slowly wastes away. The aleph, filled with all the components of his history, suggests memory itself. But it is significantly different from the cyberspace matrix. Whereas the matrix represents consensual or communal memory, the aleph represents personal memory. It is self-contained, and functions without having to be jacked into the matrix. Like Kumi, Bobby discovers he must enter, confront, and make peace with his past. He must come to terms with his relationship to Angie and 3Jane to find contentment.

Both Bobby and Gentry learn to live increasingly spiritual and private existences. Unlike the soapbox evangelist in the Sprawl at which Mona (and Gibson) laughs, both Bobby's and Gentry's quests for a transcendental signified are taken seriously. Bobby searches the aleph for an answer to why the matrix changed following

Wintermute's union with Neuromancer. Gentry searches for the shape of the matrix that he believes will in turn lead him to its meaning. Both computer cowboys look for a metanarrative, an overarching story that will lend their lives significance. They look for an answer to the cosmos. At the same time that Gibson announces this spiritual dimension to existence, however, he also undercuts it in at least two ways. First, he indicates that the loa or subprograms have begun fading in the matrix. The spiritual has begun disappearing at the very moment it is sought, as though to seek after the religious is somehow to be doomed to miss it. Moreover, Continuity's attempt to create a new spiritual order fails. Second, Gibson doesn't allow either of his characters actually to attain the goals of their respective quests. The novel ends with Finn promising Bobby enlightenment "in a New York minute," while Gentry stays behind at the Factory to figure out what has just happened. Gibson thereby reminds the reader that the goal of the quest is the quest itself, that at best one must yet again deal with pieces in the absence of wholes.

Bobby, Gentry, and Slick are artists. They privilege the imagination while minimizing the material world. Bobby feels most alive within the aleph, Gentry within the matrix, and Slick with his robots. They share another trait: each has abandoned some form of community in order to pursue his art, realizing at some level that public creation is impure creation. Angie and Mona, on the other hand, never arrive at such a discovery. For them, art has become a business, a way of making good money. Their stories lead to a consideration of another central theme in the novel: public art as commercial sellout. This theme grows directly from the Hollywood world Gibson experienced while writing this novel, and it serves as a warning both to him and to his readers.

Angie's and Mona's storylines, each of which contains nine chapters, are so interdependent that they should be discussed together. The first focuses on events culminating in Angie's kidnapping, death, and marriage to Bobby in the aleph. The second involves Mona Lisa's education regarding the horrific nature of the Sense/Net world. After remaining free of the loa or subprograms for three years, Angie is approached by Mamman Brigitte, most ancient of the dead, with a warning that someone has tried reworking the biochips in her brain so that most of the loa or subprograms can't reach her; this someone is Continuity, which has attempted without success to restructure her biochips to bring about a new order of AIs in the matrix. Angie leaves her Malibu beach house, where she has been recuperating from an addiction to a drug that allows her to "feel normal" (a drug supplied by Continuity as part of its scheme), and heads to the Sprawl to begin a new simstim project. There she is kidnapped by Molly, taken to Dog Solitude, and sacrificed by the loa or subprograms so that she may join Bobby; the exact reasons for this are unclear. Behind the kidnapping and sacrifice are two people. Robin Lanier, her leading man, is in league with 3Jane; he is jealous of Angie for her simstim fame while 3Jane is jealous of Angie for her central position in the matrix. Mona's plot is less complicated. One of Swain's men flies Mona and her pimp-boyfriend Eddy from Florida to the Sprawl, where Mona undergoes plastic surgery and becomes Angie's double. Eddy is murdered. Following her deal with the loa or subprograms, Molly breaks into Mona's room, takes her to the abduction site, kidnaps Angie, and drives them to Dog Solitude, where Mona becomes Angie's replacement.

The commerical universe of Sense/Net thus devalues selfhood by manipulating identity. While it is not actually responsible for initiating the metamorphosis of Mona into Angie, it does look the other way when that metamorphosis occurs because it perceives that to do so is in its best financial interests. Consequently, value in this novel falls not on who characters actually are, nor what they do, but on who they can seem to be. Like Angie and Mona, most play roles rather than living honest lives. Reinforcing this idea, disguises proliferate. Kumi wears her mother's mask, while Molly pretends to be Sally Shears. Danielle Stark, the interviewer, appears to be in her thirties, but in fact is closer to ninety. Even the New Suzuki Envoy Hotel seems to be something it's not, a mountain from the Hudson Valley region that comes complete with engineered strains of flora and robotic fauna. The artificial and the real are fused and confused. Such a notion echoes that of philosopher Jean Baudrillard who argues in "The Precession of Simulacra," his seminal essay on postmodernism, that mass media have neutralized the idea of "reality" in our culture. They have done this, according to Baudrillard, by generating so many re-presentations and false presentations that the concept of "the real thing" has been lost.

Through advertising, media hype, television, and so forth, these simulacra of "reality" have taken the place of the authentic. They have finally not only begun to mask "the real thing," but have also even begun to mask the absence of "the real thing."[3]

Appropriately, the title of *Mona Lisa Overdrive* looks back to Leonardo da Vinci's 1503 painting that has become an icon of Western humanism, beauty, and pure art. Leonardo labored three years on this tribute to the wife of a prominent Florentine citizen. His subject's famous suggestion of a smile embodies Baldassare Castiglione's norm of aristocratic behavior, *sprezzatura*, a word that derives from *disprezzo* or *disdain*. As Frederick Hartt comments, this is not the condescending disdain for others, "but the serene unconcern about economic realities or financial display that often denotes inheritors of wealth and power."[4] Leonardo's Mona Lisa thereby displays disinterest before the commercial world. Gibson's Mona Lisa, on the other hand, displays the opposite. She can only conceptualize her world in monetary terms. By adding the high-tech word *overdrive* to the name *Mona Lisa*, Gibson disfigures and devalues Leonardo's icon. He hollows out the Western tradition in the same way that Kumi's ghost, Colin, is hollowed out so that its data on Shakespeare and Dickens can be replaced by defense strategies. A name associated with humanism is applied to a novel whose core concerns corporate finances. A name associated with authentic beauty is applied to a novel whose core concerns the multiplication of simulacra. Its protagonist's name becomes a kind of bad joke played on the Western heritage. Pure art has become a sixteen-year-old nude dancer and prostitute from Cleveland, Ohio, who inherits the wealth and power of a simstim star. Pure art has become a pale re-presentation of the genuine. The Sense/Net universe of power games, designer drugs, and vicious innuendo transforms art into a business where form rather than content is important. Fittingly, the Austrian director Hans Becker no longer needs real people to make his documentary on the Tessier-Ashpool empire. Impure art no longer needs the human to be financially successful.

Two motifs emphasize this theme of art as commercial sellout: books and vampires. Registers of tradition and serious ideas, books have become devalued in Gibson's futureworld. Mona, the essence of the Sense/Net cosmos, can't read. Her father kept remnants of books in plastic baggies, and when he read to her, he evinced "a kind of hesitation in his voice, like a man trying to play an instrument he hasn't picked up in a long time" (chap. 11). Gentry, another eccentric, keeps ancient books as well, an act seen as quaint by those around him. These two men suggest an antiquated system of interpretation and values. In the Sense/Net universe, tradition and serious ideas are viewed as no more than curious cultural detritus. Images of vampires, the second dominant motif, run throughout the novel. Little Bird, for instance, worries that Bobby might be one, while Kumi believes there is "something vampiric" about her room at Swain's (chap. 2). The Jack Draculas who try to mug Kumi appear twice. Related to this, eating and sucking imagery is also prevalent. From Slick's point of view, the aleph literally feeds on Bobby's brain. "You don't have to be scared of Swain," Molly tells Kumi, "Yanaka could have him for breakfast" (chap. 9). Kumi's mother tells her that old men "suck our breath away. Your father sucks my breath away" (chap. 34). Sense/Net in particular, and the corporate world in general, has transfigured through the course of Gibson's novels from wasp nest, to intricate machine, to vampiric entity that drains the life from the living. Yet this world has a very real allure for such characters as Angie, Mona, and Hilton Swift.

The conclusion of *Mona Lisa Overdrive* enacts the ambivalence Gibson feels toward this cosmos. Emblematically, it registers the often contradictory impulses between the pressures of publishing financially successful novels and the need to produce interesting art. The first of these impulses is embodied by the sense of completion and fulfillment that pervades the last third of the text. "Order and accord are again established," as Kumi's father asserts (chap. 41). Peace is made among the Yakuza in Japan, as well as between Kumi and her father. Angie learns to forgive 3Jane. In a disconcertingly idyllic last chapter, Angie and Bobby are happily married after death, a futuristic version of Catherine and Heathcliff in *Wuthering Heights*. Molly, the embodiment of cyberpunk consciousness, retires as mercenary. All of this seems to add up to Gibson's attempt, as he explains it, to "find my way into the mainstream of fiction" and "*out* of [science fiction] without losing a sense of what it is I'm doing."[5] Yet at the same time that Gibson speaks of moving away from science fiction and toward mainstream literature, he also writes his fourth, longest, and most complex science fiction novel, *The Difference Engine* (1991), with Bruce Sterling. No longer set in cyberspace, it revolves around an alternate universe where the Victorian inventor Charles Babbage builds a computer early in the nineteenth century.

The need to produce innovative art is embodied by a number of disjunctive components also at work in *Mona Lisa Overdrive*. Not only does Gibson once more give the reader a series of highly complex interconnected plotlines, but he also continues to experiment with technique and language, as when in chapter eighteen he attempts mimicking Slick's short-term memory lapses on the page. One must also keep in mind that Bobby and Angie's "marriage" in a "France that isn't France" (chap. 45) may be read parodically, that the cosmos of the aleph may serve as a ludicrous image of the conventional novel that exists in a radically different world than that of Dog Solitude. As Slick reminds the reader, the cosmos of the aleph is "*not a place . . . , it only feels like it.*" Rather, it feels more like a "fairytale" (chap. 24). At the instant Gibson gives the reader a traditionally happy ending, he also reminds the reader of the artificiality of such simplistic and innocent structures. Moreover, on the last two pages of the novel, Gibson once more raises the possibility of intergalactic cyberspace, hence echoing the close of *Neuromancer*. He thereby generates inconclusiveness at the very moment of apparent conclusion (which, however, calculatedly cries out for yet another financially successful sequel).[6]

Given the relative tameness and complacency of *Mona Lisa Overdrive*, the reader must wonder about the future of Gibson's work.[7] What are its chances of continuing to challenge what readers take for granted about language and experience, particularly if Gibson himself claims he is "scared of being typecast if I make SF my permanent home"?[8] The answer is probably that it's still too early to tell. *Mona Lisa Overdrive* may simply be the product of a single science fiction writer of the 1980's who has suddenly achieved success and who suddenly needs to rewrite paler and paler versions of the same book to continue that success. Or it might be a literary register of an increasingly conservative era. Certainly Gibson's next book, *The Difference Engine*, enacts Manny Farber's dictum for the "termite school" of art: "termite-like, it feeds its way through walls of particularization, with no sign that the artist has any object in mind other than eating away the immediate boundaries of his art, and turning these boundaries into conditions of the next achievement."⁹ In any case, William Gibson's work will remain central to understanding of science fiction approaching the millennium, raising as it does essential questions concerning a genre that until recently has been marginalized, but that now has begun to move into a central — and perhaps therefore uninteresting — position in our culture.

Endnotes

[1] Paul Kincaid, "Mona Lisa Overdrive," *Times Literary Supplement* 12 August, 1988, 892.
[2] Leanne C. Harper, "The Culture of Cyberspace," *The Bloomsbury Review* 8.5 (September/October 1988), 30.
[3] See Jean Baudrillard, "The Precession of Simulacra," in *Art After Modernism: Rethinking Representation*, ed. Brian Wallis (Boston: Godine, 1984).
[4] Frederick Hartt, *History of Italian Renaissance Art* (Englewood Cliffs, NJ: Prentice-Hall, 1987), 457.
[5] Larry McCaffery, "An Interview with William Gibson," *Mississippi Review* 16.2 & 3 (1988), 236.
[6] Gibson maintains that there won't be any more sequels.
[7] Gibson disagrees that *MLO* is relatively tame and complacent. Rather, he senses a certain "interstitial nastiness" in the novel. "Stylistics aside," he wrote me, "I find the implied human world here both realer and uglier [than the previous novels]."
[8] McCaffery, 236.
[9] Manny Farber, "White Elephant Art vs. Termite Art," *Negative Space* (New York: Praeger, Inc., 1971), 135-6.

Primary Bibliography

Novels:

Neuromancer. New York: Ace, 1984. The cyberpunk classic, and first in the Matrix Trilogy, about an artificial intelligence's plot to unite with its other self.

Count Zero. New York: Ace, 1986. Sequel to *N* composed of three intersecting plotlines: mercenaries extract a top research scientist from Maas Biolabs; a woman is hired to search for the originator of fake Cornell boxes; a fledgling computer hacker discovers the results of the union of the two AIs in *N*.

Mona Lisa Overdrive. New York: Bantam, 1988. Last of the Matrix Trilogy, this novel is composed of four intersecting plotlines: the daughter of a Yakuza goes into hiding in London; the fledgling computer hacker from *CZ* enters a model of the matrix; the daughter of the research scientist from *CZ* is visited by the remains of the two AIs from *N*; a young woman undergoes plastic surgery in a plot to kill the daughter of the research scientist and replace her.

The Difference Engine (with Bruce Sterling). New York: Bantam, 1991. A radical departure from cyberspace, this is Gibson's longest and most complex novel. An alternate history where an inventor builds a computer early in the nineteenth century.

Short Stories:

Burning Chrome. New York: Ace, 1986. Includes:

"Fragments of a Hologram Rose," *Unearth* (Summer 1977). Most technically experimental story about a failed love affair in the future.

"The Gernsback Continuum," *Universe 11*, ed. Terry Carr (New York: Doubleday, 1981). The future imagined by the 1930s seeps into the present.

"The Belonging Kind" (with John Shirley), *Shadows 4*, ed. Charles L. Grant (New York: Doubleday, 1981). A linguist uncovers reptilian creatures masquerading as humans.

"Johnny Mnemonic," *Omni* May 1981. A low-life stores espionage data for a gangster on a chip implanted in his brain. Sprawl Series. One of Gibson's best.

"Hinterlands," *Omni* October 1981. Life on a space station designed to debrief astronauts returning from another dimension.

"Burning Chrome," *Omni* July 1982. Sprawl Series. Proto-*Neuromancer*, about computer hackers invading ("burning") the network of a woman named Chrome.

"Red Start, Winter Orbit" (with Bruce Sterling), *Omni* July 1983. A "Heinlein dream" in which the first man on Mars finds the government has decided to scrap the space station he has lived on for twenty years.

"New Rose Hotel," *Omni* July 1984. Last in the Sprawl Series, and a blueprint for *CZ*, a story about corporate defection and deception.

"Dogfight" (with Michael Swanwick), *Omni* July 1985. A petty thief does battle with a 3-D video involving antique planes.

"The Winter Market" *Interzone, Vancouver Magazine,* and *Stardate* Spring 1986. A metaphor for the rock'n'roll world about an unbalanced and diseased woman with Hollywood aspirations who makes it big with simstim.

Secondary Bibliography

Aldiss, Brian W. *Trillion Year Spree: The History of Science Fiction.* London: Gollancz Ltd., 1986. Brief entry on Gibson that salutes his dazzling style and attacks his amoral characters.

Alkon, Paul. "Deus Ex Machina in William Gibson's Cyberpunk Trilogy." Paper delivered at Fiction 2000 conference at the University of Leeds, June 28-July 1, 1989. Gibson combines such genres as the gothic and the mimetic in a Bakhtinian dialogic combination.

Benford, Gregory. "Is Something Going On?" *Mississippi Review* 16.2 & 3 (1988): 18-23. Assault upon cyberpunk as more marketing strategy than literary movement.

Breton, André. "Surrealism." *The Modern Tradition.* Ed. Richard Ellmann and Charles Feidelson, Jr. New York: Oxford UP, 1965. The proto-cyberpunk surrealist manifesto.

Brin, David. "Starchilde Harold, Revisited." *Mississippi Review* 16.2 & 3 (1988): 23-27. Ambivalent statement about cyberpunk's style, vision, and tendency toward self-promotion.

Brunner, John. *The Shockwave Rider.* New York: Ballantine, 1975. Key proto-cyberpunk novel heavily influenced by Toffler and featuring computer hackers.

Csicsery-Ronay, Istvan. "Cyberspace." *American Book Review* 10.6 (January-February 1989): 7. Mildly negative rev. of MLO.

—————. "Cyberpunk and Neuromanticism." *Mississippi Review* 16.2 & 3 (1988): 266-78. Ambivalent interrogation of cyberpunk, which Csicsery-Ronay views as the apotheosis of postmodernism.

Delany, Samuel R. "Is Cyberpunk a Good Thing or a Bad Thing?" *Mississippi Review* 16.2 & 3 (1988): 28-35. Intelligent weighing of pros and cons concerning the cyberpunk controversy, with reference to Gibson in particular.

Disch, Thomas M. "Mona Lisa Overdrive." *New York Times Book Review* 11 December 1988: 23. Generally positive rev. of *MLO*.

Devillers, Carole. "Haiti's Voodoo Pilgrimages: Of Spirits and Saints." *National Geographic* March 1985: 395-410. Source for much of the voodoo material Gibson used in *CZ* and *MLO*.

Dorsey, Candas Jane. "Beyond Cyberspace." *Books in Canada* June-July 1988: 11-13. Fine general profile of Gibson.

Farber, Manny. "White Elephant Art and Termite Art." *Negative Space* New York: Praeger, 1971. One of the few essays Gibson claims directly influenced his aesthetics.

Gaiman, Neil. "Loving the Alien." *Time Out* 1-8 June 1988: 14. Brief interview focusing on *MLO* and *TDE*

Gilmore, Mikal. "The Rise of Cyberpunk." *Rolling Stone* (4 December, 1986): 77. Predictable intro to Gibson and his universe.

Hamburg, Victoria. "The King of Cyberpunk." *Interview* January 1989: 84-87, 91. Good interview focusing on *MLO* and Gibson's sense of the future.

Harper, Leanne C. "The Culture of Cyberspace." *The Bloomsbury Review* 8.5 (September/October 1988): 16-17, 30. Strong interview focusing on influences and *TDE*.

Kelly, Kevin. "Cyberpunk Era." *Whole Earth Review* Summer 1989: 78-83. Pastiche of earlier reviews of Gibson and a good cyberpunk reading list by Richard Kadrey.

Kessel, John. "The Humanist Manifesto." *Science Fiction Eye* 1.1 (Winter 1987): 52-56. Provocative "humanist" response to cyberpunk.

Kincaid, Paul. "Mona Lisa Overdrive." *Times Literary Supplement* August 12 1988: 892. Luke-warm rev. of *MLO*, indicative of the novel's critical reception.

Leary, Timothy. "High Tech High Life — William Gibson & Timothy Leary In Conversation." *Mondo 2000* 7 (Fall 1989): 58-64. Good discussion of William Burroughs, Douglas Adams, Thomas Pynchon, characterization, and drugs by the man whom Leary calls "Quark of the Decade."

MacNair, Marian. "Mainframe Voodoo." *Montreal Mirror* (7-20 April, 1989): 23. Standard profile of Gibson and his work through *MLO*.

Maddox, Tom. "Cobra, She Said: An Interim Report on the Fiction of William Gibson." *Fantasy Review* 9.4 (April 1986): 46-48. One of the first more serious critical looks into the essence of Gibson's fiction.

McCaffery, Larry. "An Interview with William Gibson." *Mississippi Review* 16.2 & 3 (1988): 217-36. Excellent and broad interview with much emphasis on influences, early career, and aesthetics.

─────, ed. "The Cyberpunk Controversy." *Mississippi Review* 16.2 & 3 (1988). First-rate and balanced special issue on cyberpunk in general, Gibson in particular. Essays, stories, and comments by SF writers such as Delany, Rucker, and Sterling; critics such as Brooks Landon, George Slusser, and Istvan Csicsery-Ronay.

─────, ed. *Storming the Reality Studio: A Casebook of Cyberpunk and Postmodern Fiction*. Durham: Duke VP, 1991. The best collection of essays, fiction, and poetry to date by and about cyberpunkers and postmodernists such as J.G. Ballard, Don Dehillo, Jean-François Lyotard and Brian McHale. A must read for those in the field.

McGuirk, Carol. "The 'New' Romancers: Science Fiction Innovators from Gernsback to Gibson." Paper delivered at Fiction 2000 conference at the University of Leeds, June 28-July 1, 1989. Places Gibson in the context of hard and soft SF.

Nicholas, Joseph and Judith Hanna. "William Gibson." *Interzone* 1.13 (1985): 17-18. Good early interview which by now covers familiar territory.

Pohl, Frederick. Untitled. *Mississippi Review* 16.2 & 3 (1988): 46. Attack upon cyberpunk's disagreeable characters.

Porush, David. "Cybernauts in Cyberspace: William Gibson's *Neuromancer.*" *Aliens: The Anthropology of Science Fiction.* Ed. George C. Slusser and Eric Rabkin. Carbondale: Southern Illinois UP, 1987. Exploration of distinction between man and machine, with particularly interesting material on scientific advances in real cyberspace.

Pynchon, Thomas. *Gravity's Rainbow.* New York: Viking, 1973. The cyberpunk classic.

Rirdan, Danny. "The Works of William Gibson." *Foundation* 43 (Summer 1988): 36-46. One of the first in-depth evaluations of Gibson's fiction, with some fine work on style and apparent slips in Gibson's knowledge of technology (which Gibson has tried to refute).

Shippey, Tom and George Slusser, eds. *Fiction 2000: Cyberpunk and the Future of Narrative.* Athens: U Georgia P, 1992. Excellent collection of essays on cyberpunk from the Leeds conference, 1989.

Sterling, Bruce. "Preface." *Mirrorshades: The Cyberpunk Anthology.* New York: Arbor House, 1986. The cyberpunk manifesto by the self-proclaimed cyberpunk spokesperson in the first and definitive collection of short cyberpunk fiction.

Tallant, Robert. *Voodoo In New Orleans.* New York: Collier, 1962. Gibson read this book, first published in 1946, when a teenager in Virginia. A major source for his voodoo material.

Tatsumi, Takayuki. "An Interview with William Gibson." *Science Fiction Eye* 1.1 (Winter 1987): 6-17. Strong interview with Gibson in which Tom Maddox and others play a major role.

Toffler, Alvin. *The Third Wave.* New York: William Morrow, 1980. Although Gibson never read it, Bruce Sterling refers to this as the Bible of cyberpunk. A generally optimistic sociological study of the future that argues the new society will be based on decentralization and fluidity.

Index

A

Acker, Kathy: 1, 13, 16
Action precedes essence: 69-70, 99-100
Aesthetics of the unpleasant: 38
Aldiss, Brian: 13, 28
Algren, Nelson: 70
Alkon, Paul: 34-35, 91-92, 101
Ambiguity: 36, 51, 66, 72
Anderson, Laurie: 13, 16
Animal: 26
Anthology: 12
Art-as-business: 30-32, 92-95, 104, 107-110
Artificial Kid, The (Sterling): 13
Artist: 58, 59, 68, 93, 94
Artist figure: 30, 31, 58, 59-61, 67, 68, 93-95, 103, 106, 107
As I Lay Dying (Faulkner): 89
Asimov, Isaac: 20
Assemblage: 31
Atrocity Exhibition, The (Ballard): 7, 19
Autism: 72, 73

B

Babbage, Charles: 111
Ballard, J. G.: 5, 7, 13, 19
Barthelme, Donald: 2, 28, 32, 36
Barthes, Roland: 33
Baudelaire, Charles-Pierre: 38
Baudrillard, Jean: 18, 108, 109
Bear, Greg: 13
Beast Within, The (Mora): 77
Beckett, Samuel: 28
"Belonging Kind, The" (and John Shirley): 25, 27, 50, 51, 60
Benford, Gregory: 16, 28
Bester, Alfred: 7
Betrayal: 52, 54, 57, 58, 86, 89
Biblical: 72, 78, 87

Big Sleep, The (Chandler): 81
Blade Runner: 8, 13
Blood Music (Bear): 13
Blues, the: 8
Boccioni, Umberto: 15
Body: 60
Book motif: 109, 110
Borges, Jorge Luis: 49
Bowie, David: 13, 16
Bradbury, Ray: 5
Braque, Georges: 31
Breton, André: 30
"Bride Stripped Bare by Her Bachelors, Even, The" (DuChamps): 31
Brin, David: 16, 35
Brontë, Emily: 30
Brunner, John: 13, 18, 27, 39
Burgess, Anthony: 15
Burke, Edmund: 78, 79
"Burning Chrome": 6, 8, 15, 22, 26, 36, 37, 51, 54-58, 63
Burning Chrome : 47-61, 89
Burroughs, William: 5, 7, 31, 32, 51
Byronic: 30, 67

C

Cadigan, Pat: 13
Campbell, John: 49
Caramello, Charles: 18
Carpenter, John: 8
Carr, Terry: 63
Carroll, Lewis: 74
Castiglione, Baldassare: 109
Chandler, Raymond: 28, 51, 81
Characterization: 26-32, 69, 85-86, 88-89
Chronos: 73-74, 88
Clockwork Orange, A (Burgess): 15
Cognitive estrangement: 11
Collage: *See also* Assemblage: 31, 32, 93-94, 99
Colors, use of: 37
"Coming Attraction" (Leiber): 74

Conclusion: 80, 91, 110
Conrad, Joseph: 54
"Cool It Down" (Reed): 8
Cooper, James Fenimore: 28
Cornell: 30, 31, 85, 87, 92
Cornell, Joseph: 93, 94
Corporate: 110
Corporation: 91
Cosmic unity: 67
Count Zero : 3, 6, 8, 15-16, 23, 29, 31, 33, 39-40, 56, 67, 77, 81, 85-101, 103, 104, 105
Cronenberg, David: 8
Crying of Lot 49, The (Pynchon): 52, 96-97
Csicsery-Ronay, Istvan: 1-2, 12, 16, 17
Cubism: 31
Cybernetic sublime: 78-79
Cyberpunk: 1, 2, 5, 6, 8, 12-19
Cyberspace: 3, 8, 9, 22-24, 29, 30, 35, 36, 48,54, 58, 59, 60, 64, 66-68, 71, 73-75, 88, 90-91, 97-101, 103, 106, 111

D

Dadaism: 31-32, 94
Dali, Salvador: 30
Darwinism: 92
Davis, Grania: 22
Daydream Nation (Sonic Youth): 1
De Haven, Tom: 1
Deconstruction: 101
Defamiliarization: 11
Delany, Samuel: 7, 13, 19, 74
Demolished Man, The (Bester): 7
Descartes, René: 17, 70
Detail, use of: 36-37, 51
Devillers, Carole: 98-101
Devo: 13
Dhalgren (Delany): 19
Dick, Phillip K.: 13
Difference Engine, The (and Bruce Sterling): 111
Di Filippo, Paul: 13

Disch, Thomas: 1
Dog Soldiers: 8
"Dogfight" (and Michael Swanwick): 25, 29, 58-60
Duchamp: 31-2, 68

E

Eastwood, Clint: 74
Easy Travel to Other Planets (Mooney): 7, 52
Eclipse (Shirley): 13
Effinger, George Alec: 13
Eliot, T.S.: 38
Ellison, Harlan: 13
Empire of the Senseless (Acker): 1
Ending: 80-82, 91-92, 107, 110-112
England: 105
Epic qualities: 64, 68, 85
Epistemological, instability of: 25, 49, 79-81, 100-101
Ernst, Max: 30, 94
Erziehungsroman : 33, 89, 92, 104, 107-108
Escape from New York (Carpenter): 8
Expressionism: 15, 30
Eye motif: 15

F

Fantastic, prescence of the: 35, 79-80, 100-101
Farber, Manny: 38, 111-112
Faulkner, William: 20, 28, 66, 89-90
Faust figure: 67, 76, 90
Federman, Raymond: 7, 19
Female Man, The (Russ): 74
Filippo Tommaso Marinetti: 15
Film Noir : 28
Filmic qualities: 36
Fleming, Victor: 67
Foundation trilogy (Asimov): 20
"Fragments of a Hologram Rose" 5, 21, 26, 47-48, 54, 58, 80, 89
Frankenstein (Shelley): 76-77
Frankenstein motif: 76-77, 86-87
Free will: 71-72, 96, 105
French Symbolists: 94

Frontera (Shiner): 13
Futurism : 2, 15-16

G

gaming: 39-40
gangster heist plot: 54, 63-64, 89-90
García Márquez, Gabriel: 73
Gaudí, Antonmi: 21
gender questions: 74-75, 79, 96-97
"Gernsback Continuum, The ": 25, 27, 48-50
Gernsback, Hugo: 49
Gibson, William:
  popularity: 1-2, 12
  critical reception: 1-2
  danger of trendiness: 2, 16-17
  ignorance of technology: 2, 16-17
  biography: 4-6
  international imagination: 6-7
  intertextual imagination: 7-9
  influences: 7-9
  as postmodernist: 9-10
  as realist: 9-10, 35
  extrapolition: 9
Goethe, Johann Wolfgang von: 30, 67
Goldberg, Rube: 38
Golding, William: 3, 52
Gomi no sensei : 21, 31-32, 35-36, 51, 60, 93
Gothicqualities of fiction: 21, 23-24, 33, 72, 94
Gravity's Rainbow: 7, 26, 64, 69, 81
Gray, Alasdair: 19
grotechsque: 77
grotesque: 33, 53

H

"Haiti's Voodoo Pilgrimages,: (Devillers) 98-101
Hard-boiled detective novel: 33, 35, 68
Hammett, Dashiell: 7-8, 28, 51
hard SF's: 7
Hartt, Frederick: 109
Hegel, Georg Wilheim Friedrich: 18

Heinlein, Robert: 5, 55-56
Hemingway, Ernest: 2, 28
"Hinterlands": 53
Homer: 64, 67
Hughes, Howard: 91
Human-as-beast: 26, 52, 57, 77
Human-as-commodity: 57, 86
Hutcheon, Linda: 18
Huyssen, Andreas: 18
Hynde, Chrissie: 74

I

Imagism: 2
Immachination: 26
immortality: 66-67, 71, 75-76, 86-87, 106
information density: 36-37, 51
information economy: 24
invasion: 25, 50, 53, 54

J

Jackson, Rosemary: 80
Jameson, Fredric: 10
Japan: 21-22, 105
Jenson, Bruce: 1
"Johnny Mnemonic": 26, 51-53, 57, 58, 63
Joyce, James: 2, 53
Jung, Carl Gustav: 31, 49, 60

K

Kadrey, Richard: 13
Kafka: 2, 71
Kairos : 73-74, 88
Kandinsky, Wassily: 30
Kearney, Richard: 38
Kelly, James Patrick: 13
Kessel, John: 16
Kincaid, Paul: 103
Kubrick, Stanley: 66, 67, 76

L

Laidlaw, Marc: 13
La Mettrie, Julian Offray de: 70, 71
Lanark (Gray): 19
Laurel and Hardy: 38
Lawrence, D. H.: 28, 74
Lazarus: 87
Leary, Timothy: 14
Lee, Bruce: 74
LeGuin, Ursula K.: 5, 63
Leiber, Fritz: 74
Lisberger, Steven: 8, 76
Lord of the Flies: 3, 52
Lucas, George: 20
Lyotard, Jean François: 18

M

McCaffery, Larry: 16
McGuirk, Carol: 7, 49, 74
McHale, Brian: 18, 19
MacLean, Paul D.: 29
Maddox, Tom: 9, 13, 54
Magic: 35, 72, 78-80
Mallarmé, Stéphane: 94
Man With the Golden Arm, The (Algren): 70
Manipulation: 52, 54-55, 57, 58, 71-72
Marinetti, Filippo Tommaso: 15
Marx, Karl: 18
Mass media: 8, 23, 88, 92, 108-109
Max Headroom: 13
Maximalism: 51
Melville, Herman: 28, 30
Memories: 56, 89
Memory: 23-24, 48, 56, 67, 88, 89, 105-106
Metamorphosis: 68, 79-80, 87, 108
Metaphors, use of: 36-38, 57, 74, 77, 96
Milton, John: 92
Mind/body dualism: 23-24, 48, 58-59, 60, 73, 88, 106
Mindplayers (Cadigan): 13

Minimalism: 2
Mirror motif: 14, 87
Mirrorshades: 13
Mirrorshades: The Cyberpunk Anthology (Sterling): 12-13
Mona Lisa Overdrive: 3, 20, 21, 24, 26, 29, 31, 33, 36, 37, 40, 57, 60, 81, 88, 92, 93, 96, 98, 100, 103
Mooney, Ted: 7, 39, 52
Mora, Phillipe: 77
Multinationals: 24-25, 52-53, 56, 57, 71-72, 91, 95-96, 105, 110
MTV: 13, 36

N

Naked Lunch (Burroughs): 7
Naturalism: 70
Neo-Gothic: 21
Neuromancer: 1, 2, 3, 4, 6, 8, 12, 25, 26, 28, 29, 30, 31, 34, 37, 52, 56, 60, 68, 85, 88, 89, 90, 91, 93, 95, 97, 111
"New Rose Hotel": 6, 24, 31, 51, 56-59
New Wave: 13
Nietzsche, Freidrich: 30
Normalcy, suspicion of: 49-50, 80-81
Nova (Delany): 7

O

Odyssey (Homer) 64
One Hundred Years of Solitude (García Márquez) 73
Ontology , instability of: 25, 49, 53-54, 81, 100-101
Ovid 79-80, 87

P

Paradise Lost (Milton): 92
Patriarchal system: 96-97, 104-105
Pauline, Mark: 13, 60
Peel, Emma: 74
Philosophical Enquiry, A (Burke): 78-79
Picasso, Pablo: 4, 31
Piranesi, Giovanni Battista: 21, 30
Plagiarism: 7

Pla(y)giarism (Federman): 7
Poe, Edgar Alan: 94
Poetic language: 36-37, 100
Pohl, Frederick: 28
Pollock, Jackson: 30
Pollution: 21
popularity: 12
Porush, David: 22, 68
Postmodernism: 17-19, 32, 33, 38-39, 60-61, 64, 82, 93, 99-101, 108-109
"Precession of Simulacra, The" (Baudillard): 108
Pushkin, Alexander: 30
Pynchon, Thomas: 1, 2, 5, 7, 14, 24, 26, 27, 28, 32, 33, 36, 40, 50, 51, 64, 71, 79, 89, 95, 96

Q

Quest Motif: 64, 67, 68, 75-79, 85-87, 92-93, 97, 106-107

R

Rauschenberg, Robert: 31
Reader's Role: 33-41, 86, 90, 100-101
"Red Star, Winter Orbit" (and Bruce Sterling): 24, 55-56
Reed, Lou: 8
Relativity of perception: 80, 87, 89
Religion: 22-23, 35, 53-54, 77-79, 91, 93, 97-101, 106-107
Renaissance comedy: 80-81
Reptilian-Complex: 29
Revenge tragedy: 64
"Rikki Don't Lose that Number": 8
Rirdan, Danny: 3, 36
Rucker, Rudy: 5, 13
Russ, Joanna: 63, 74

S

Sanity: 77
Sartre, Jean-Paul: 66
Schnabel, Julian: 21
Science Fiction: 10, 11-12, 20, 49, 55-56, 68, 79-80, 110-112
Scott, Ridley: 8, 16
Selfhood: 7, 25-26, 28, 51, 52, 57-58, 68-69, 73, 79, 87, 94, 108
Self-reflexitivity: 49

Seneca: 64
Sex Pistols: 9
Shakespeare, William: 109
Shelley, Mary: 76-77
Shiner, Lewis: 4, 9, 13, 70
Shirley, John: 5, 13, 50
Shklovsky, Victor: 11
Simulacra: 26
Slusser, George: 29
Soft SF's: 7
Software (Rucker): 13
Sonic Youth: 1
Sound and the Fury, The (Faulkner): 66
Sprezzatura : 109
Springsteen, Bruce: 8
Star Wars (Lucas): 20, 81
Steely Dan: 8
Sterling, Bruce: 6, 9, 12, 13, 26, 47, 49, 51, 55, 111
Stone, Robert: 7-8, 63
Sturgeon, Theodore: 5
Style: 28, 34-41, 48, 51, 63-64, 89-90
"Sunday Morning" (Reed)
Surrealism: 30, 94, 102
Survival instinct: 27
Survival Research Laboratories 13, 60
Suvin, Darko: 11-12
Swanwick, Michael 58

T

Tallant, Robert: 102
Techno-centaur: 37, 53, 54, 58, 68-69, 86
Technology: 2-3, 7, 14, 23, 26, 29, 35, 37, 40, 68-72, 78-79, 86, 100
Tennyson, Lord Alfred: 67
Termite Art: 38-39
Thiher, Allen: 18
Thin Man, The (Hammett): 7
Third Wave, The (Toffler): 6, 17
Tithonus: 87
"Tlön, Uqbar, Orbis Tertius" (Borges): 49
Todorov, Tzvetan: 79, 100

Toffler, Alvin: 6-7, 17-18
Tron (Lisberger): 8, 76
Truffaut, François: 38
Turing, A.M.: 70
"Twilight" (Campbell): 49
Twofold Vibration, The (Federman): 19
2001: A Space Odyssey (Kubrick): 66, 67, 76

U

Ulysses- figure: 53, 65-66, 67, 81, 92, 97-98
Unity of opposites: 67, 75-78, 98

V

Vampire Motif: 37, 109-110
Vattimo, Gianni: 18
Velvet Underground, The: 8
Victorianism: 94, 111
Videodrome (Cronenberg) 8, 13
Vonnegut, Kurt: 26
Voodoo: 22, 35, 40, 80-81, 90-91, 93, 97-102, 105, 106
Voodoo In New Orleans (Tallant): 102

W

"Walk on the Wildside" (Reed): 8
Westerns: 33, 35
White Elephant Art: 38-39
Wilde, Alan: 18
"Winter Market, The ": 8, 26, 30, 31, 59, 93, 94
Wizard of Oz, The (Fleming): 67, 73
Wuthering Heights (Brontë): 110

Z

Zelazny, Roger: 63